The Coach's Advantage: Offensive Line Fundamentals

Tim Nunez

ISBN-13: 978-1-58518-999-1
ISBN-10: 1-58518-999-5
Library of Congress Control Number: 2006933851
Cover design: Bean Creek Studio
Book layout: Bean Creek Studio
Front cover photo credits: Courtesy of The University of Texas

Coaches Choice
P.O. Box 1828
Monterey, CA 93942
www.coacheschoice.com

This book is dedicated to all of my former players. A coach is nothing without players, and my life would not be the same without all of the fine players that molded me and changed my life. I have been rewarded with the privilege of watching you all grow into men. As your coach, my goal was to shape you into the best players possible, but it was even more important to me to help shape you into the best men, the best Christians, the best husbands, and the best fathers you could be. Thank you for sharing your talents and your lives with me.

I also dedicate this book to my wife, Ellen. A man has to have something to believe in, something to do, and someone to love. I struck it rich with a God that blessed me many times over with a profession in which I could not wait to immerse myself every day and the gift of such a special woman. I cannot put into words what you have meant to me. I am a better man, a better Christian, a better father, a better coach, and a better husband because of you. I love you.

Dedication

Acknowledgments

Football has been my passion for many years. I consider myself lucky that it has also been my career. This manual is a product of the lessons I learned over my football career, which has spanned three decades. I could never have had the success I had as a coach without the support and shared knowledge of many people. Likewise this book would still be a ratty collection of notes, presentations, and scribblings if it weren't for some wonderful people. For that reason, I'd like to offer my deepest gratitude to the following folks:

- High school coaches—Thanks to all of the coaches who shared their ideas with me and helped me to become a better coach. A special thanks to all of the coaches in Texas, Louisiana, and West Virginia for your hospitality and kindness. You made each stop extra special.

- Larry Zierlin—I knew from the early days at Tulane University that I wanted to coach the offensive line. It was my greatest desire to build an O-line of which you could be proud. Thanks for the countless hours you spent with me.

- Howard Mudd—My visits to you in Kansas City, Seattle, and Indianapolis all helped me improve my coaching. Thank you.

- Emily Jenkins—How you were put into my life only God knows. Your skills that turned random thoughts into this book are awe-inspiring.

- Dwayne, Jake, Jame, Mark, and Lori—You loved me when I did not always deserve it. You continue to make me proud.

- Dwayne—Having a son follow in your footsteps is an incredible experience. Having a son follow in your footsteps and exceed you is the greatest compliment anyone can ever pay a father.

- Jim Bob Helduser—You gave me the opportunity to live my dream coaching the offensive line. Thanks for allowing me to bring the dream to life.

- Greg Davis—After a few years of coaching with someone, you're bound to become friends. After 15 years of coaching with you, I consider you one of my greatest friends.

- Doug Ethridge—Thank you for giving me that first high school coaching job and the state championship. More importantly, thank you for shaping me into the best possible coach I could be.

- Greg Olejack—I showed up in Kansas in 1981 when you were still a newlywed. Thanks for your friendship, and thanks to Meg for allowing us to continue the friendship.

- Steve Green—Max has a great friend in you, and I thank him for putting us together and I thank you for your direction and guidance.

- Wade Philips—For many years of friendship and your kind assistance in writing the foreword.

- Leonard Davis, Robbie Doane, Derrick Dockery, and Mike Williams—Thanks for your time and energy on the photos for the book and the video.

- Bob Pruett—What a great two years! A national championship, a MAC championship, and the opportunity to work with so many great players and coaches.

Contents

As a defensive coordinator and head coach in the NFL, I've spent years studying the offense. My observations have taught me valuable lessons about the offensive line, which is the foundation of offensive play. Five of 11 players make up the line, and one individual coaches all of them—a big responsibility for any team. The offensive line coach searches for tools and techniques that will translate to an advantage on the field, frustrating defensive coaches and players. To that end, any level of offensive line coach will be pleased with this manual.

The Coach's Advantage: Offensive Line Fundamentals is a tremendous tool for offensive line coaches. Rookie coaches will surely learn enough to feel more confident in their jobs, and coaches with some level of experience will pick up something to improve their coaching and their players' performance. Even coaches with a great deal of knowledge and experience will gain something more from reading this manual.

I have known Tim Nunez for many years. We played football together in high school and have remained friends throughout our coaching careers. This manual is evidence of Tim's passion for teaching and instruction. All aspects of the offensive line are well-defined and very precise. The theory in this book is solid and works on the blackboard and on the field. If I were a beginning coach, I'd study every page and take it with me to practice. Even as a seasoned coach, I found information in this book that amounted to insightful reminders of what makes the offense succeed. I know that other coaches will also find it invaluable.

— Wade Phillips
Defensive Coordinator
San Diego Chargers

Foreword

Preface

Coaching and playing the offensive line is a difficult job. As a 32-year coaching veteran, I know firsthand the difficulties the job involves. *The Coach's Advantage: Offensive Line Fundamentals* is a compilation of tips and techniques that offensive line coaches (both new coaches and veteran coaches), players, and parents can use to make the most difficult position in football a little easier.

While many football coaching manuals focus on plays, this manual focuses on the fundamentals of the offensive line. My experience has proven to me and my players that it is the fundamentals that make an unstoppable offensive line. This book is *not* a playbook, but a how-to manual on offensive line play.

For players, this book supplements your knowledge of the game. Playing the offensive line is as much mental as it is physical, as you will read in this book, and a "smart" player can use his knowledge to overcome his deficiencies in other areas. Remember: size is not everything.

For parents, this book will give you and your son an appreciation of the skills it takes to play the offensive line. And remember: not every son grows up to be the quarterback or a running back.

For coaches, this manual serves as a reference book, a book to give you ideas and to make them your own when combined with your thoughts and your techniques. When you have finished with this book, hopefully you will have markings on every page where you have improved this book, and improved the techniques of your linemen to help make them better players.

Thank you to all the hundreds of coaches that have spent time talking football with me, and allowing me to pick your brain. This manual is a compilation of those thoughts and ideas.

THE FUNDAMENTALS

Jonathan Daniel/Getty Images

Chapter One

Without mastery of the fundamentals, the offensive line is doomed to a lackluster season. Without a solid understanding of the mental and physical building blocks, well-chosen players will turn in a mediocre performance on the line. The best plays will never compensate for an offensive line that does not demonstrate and utilize proper technique. It is *technique* that wins and loses games. Offensive line coaches who understand this basic truth will fare better every season than those coaches who provide limited instruction and support in the most important areas of the game: the fundamentals.

**Technique:
Proper position
of the feet, head,
and hands**

The offensive line coach should teach his players not only the physical components of the game, but the mental aspects as well. Although what's inside a lineman's head may seem secondary to his stance or running skills, it is actually key to the success of the offensive line. The mental part of the game should be coached every day just as the physical part is coached.

The line must learn to play with one heartbeat. Even the most impressive offensive lineman is compromised if his playing partner makes mental mistakes and fails to execute his assignment properly. In such a case, even the best offensive lineman in the world begins to compensate for his partner, and as a result, his execution suffers. Developing the offensive line's mental game increases trust amongst the linemen and allows them to play with one heartbeat.

The Four C's

To be successful, members of an offensive line must learn to play with one heartbeat. The four C's are characteristics that the offensive line must develop to perform as a unit.

- *Confidence:* Players move with confidence, believing that "The only way a defender can beat me is if I make a mistake."

- *Consistency:* Players believe that repetition leads to consistency.

- *Concentration:* Players honor the mental aspects of the game as much as the physical components. Players understand that success on the line requires absolute concentration.

- *Cohesiveness:* At the line, five players instinctively play with one heartbeat, always working as one cohesive unit.

Once the four C's are imbedded into an offensive line, the individual linemen are transformed into one unit that moves and plays in sync. Players that exhibit the four C's are like the player who knows he is in great shape and doesn't worry about sprints after practice. Instead, his concentration is focused on learning and improving, not on the pain of the sprints. The four C's are a formula for competitive advantage.

Coaching Point

The Four C's of a Great Offense

- Confidence
- Consistency
- Concentration
- Cohesiveness

Think

Teaching the mental game means teaching players to think. A successful offensive lineman is constantly thinking. On every play, he runs through the answers to four questions:

■ Who?

The offensive lineman is clear on his assignment, and identifies the player he is blocking on every play.

■ When?

The major advantage that the offensive line has over the defense is the snap count. Offensive linemen must be clear about when to move to maximize this advantage

■ Where?

Every successful offensive lineman clearly understands the step, landmark, and punch required on every snap. A lineman knows without doubt that he has absolutely no chance to be successful unless he steps correctly, aligns his helmet (landmark) so that the defender will react accordingly, and uses his hands (punch) correctly to gain leverage against the defender. In this instance, the following factors are critical:

- Step—the lineman takes a pre-determined first step that puts him on a correct angle to block the defender.
- Landmark—the lineman's head is positioned on the defender so that, along with his hands, his head forms a tripod to aid in controlling the defender.
- Punch—the lineman places his hands on the defender in order to gain leverage on the defender.

■ What?

Offensive linemen understand the structure of the defense. They clearly understand the tendencies of the defense based on their alignment, and they use this information to their advantage on every play.

Tendency of the defense: What the defense is most likely to do in a given situation based on past performances

Coaching Point

On every play, the lineman knows:

- Who
- When
- Where
- What

Visualization

Visualization: Seeing the block occur before it actually happens

Many athletes understand and use the power of visualization to perfect and maintain their skill. Visualization is also key to a successful offensive line. A lineman must be able to visualize a block and the reaction of the defender to the play (this reaction can be compared to shooting ducks).

Shooting ducks: Moving at an angle to intercept a moving target

In order to shoot a duck, the hunter must aim in the direction the duck is moving, not in the direction of the duck at the moment the shot is fired. Likewise, the defender is going to react to the ball and move in the direction of the ball. A lineman must allow for movement of the defender, and block him wherever he moves. In an instant, the lineman should be able to visualize correct position of hands, helmet, and feet. Visualizing position will ensure that the lineman finds perfect body position on each play, consistently and successfully.

Perfect position: Feet, helmet, and hands aligned to execute a flawless block

To encourage visualization, the coach can ask the linemen to get into "perfect position" against the defender, and then make corrections, if needed. Linemen can then be sent to the line of scrimmage and asked to visualize the perfect position and the steps required to assume that position.

Failure

No learning occurs without failure. This statement is especially true for the offensive line. Analyzing blocking failures allows players and coaches to learn from mistakes, and to greatly improve offensive line skills.

To analyze blocking failures, every play in a game should be graded for technique and results. Technique is broken down into the fundamentals of each block: step (the position of the feet), landmark (the position of the helmet), and punch (the position of the hands).

Results must also be graded. A player may do some things wrong but still manage to complete his blocking assignment. Effort is tremendous; it overcomes everything else. Regardless of what the player does as a technician, the result of the block must be taken into consideration.

When analyzing blocking failure, the coach must emphasize technique. Players must be convinced that technique is the key to a successful block. Proper technique is the means to winning every play. When the defense beats an offensive lineman on a play, the coach needs to demonstrate how a flaw in technique resulted in the failure. Offensive players should recognize and be convinced that the only way to lose a play is to make an error in technique. Success and failure are always a result of the offensive lineman's technique. The most common causes of blocking failures include:

Mental Errors

Simply put, a mental error is blocking the wrong player. Although rare, mental errors do occur.

Angle of Departure

The first and second step off the line of scrimmage must be exactly right. Visualizing the first two steps helps players eliminate this failure.

> **Angle of departure:** The first and second step used to insure the block on the defender

Missed Snap Count

Players who understand the four C's should never miss the snap count for lack of concentration. On occasion, however, crowd noise or other factors can contribute to missing the snap count.

Loafing

Most coaches probably have little tolerance for this error. When faced with a player who loafs, a coach can appeal to the player's sense of pride. A loafing player must watch himself on tape alongside his teammates. Afterward, if his pride doesn't ignite effort on the line, the player who continues to loaf must be benched.

Coaching Point

Don't coach effort.

Loss of Base

Loss of base is a common error caused by improper position of the feet (step). Offensive linemen must learn to plant their feet correctly to maintain a sturdy base (Figure 1-1).

No Punch

Many coaches don't spend enough time coaching players on the use of their hands (punch). A lineman must be taught to throw his hands into the defender instead of cocking his hands and then throwing. The player who gets his hands inside first usually wins. The offensive lineman increases his chances of winning by using correct punch technique. The snap count has already been identified as the offensive line's major advantage; use of hands is the other. Players can block with their bodies, but "punch" gives linemen a significant advantage.

Base: The position of strength. The feet are shoulder-width apart with a toe-to-instep or toe-to-heel stagger. The weight is on the arches.

Figure 1-1. Proper base

Figure 1-2. Improper base—the feet are not staggered

Figure 1-3. Improper base—weight is unevenly distributed

Lack of Finish

Offensive line players should be consistently reminded to follow through with each block. All blocks cannot be pancakes. Sometimes all it takes to break a long run or keep the quarterback standing is a push that prevents the defender from setting his feet and making the tackle.

Coaching Point

Push with your hands and keep pushing.
At the whistle, push one more time.

Sit on the Bar Stool

Finish: Extra effort at the end of a block.

Before a lineman learns to run and shuffle, he must learn to "sit on the bar stool." Weightlifting squat and power clean lifts build power and strength in athletes. The stance used in these two lifts is the same position of strength required for a proper football stance, the bar-stool position. In the proper bar-stool position, the lineman maintains three angles in his body: the knee, the ankle, and the hip (Figure 1-4). The proper angles can be achieved by placing the ankle outside the knee and the knee outside the hip. If the knee aligns on top of the ankle, or if the hip aligns on top of the knee, a lineman will be unable to move his leg. Players achieve the three angles by using the following guidelines:

• Feet are in the same position as the stance, approximately shoulder-width apart, staggered toe to instep or toe to heel.

• Knees are slightly bent.

• Elbows are in, and fingertips are right below the eyes.

• Shoulders are back and chest is out.

Figure 1-4. Sitting on the bar stool

Stance

A sprinter explodes out of his stance using starting blocks, which give him the great start needed to win. The offensive lineman has no starting blocks, only his stance. In order to achieve the solid start required to win every play, the lineman must maintain correct position of feet and hands and correct weight distribution.

The effectiveness of every play depends upon the lineman's ability to maintain a proper stance. A strategically sound play fails if the lineman's base causes him to miss his block. A proper stance is the foundation that allows the line to excel.

Stance is classified as right-handed or left-handed. Linemen on the right side of the center assume the right-handed stance (right foot back, right hand down), and those to the left of the center assume the left-handed stance (left foot back, left hand down). In both stances, feet should be shoulder-width apart (see Figures 1-5 and 1-6).

In both stances, the outside foot is placed slightly behind the inside foot with toes pointing out. The stagger varies from toe to instep or toe to heel of the inside foot, depending upon where the player feels most comfortable and upon the lineman's height—the longer the legs, the greater the stagger.

Stagger: The front-to-back position of the feet.

The player should concentrate his weight over his arches by pulling his knees together. Doing so shifts the weight to the arches allowing the lineman to move efficiently.

Figure 1-5. Right-handed stance

Figure 1-6. Left-handed stance

Lateral movement: Any sideways movement.

Coaching Point

A stance that is too narrow reduces the player's stability (Figure 1-7).
A stance that is too wide hinders the player's lateral movement (Figure 1-8).

Figure 1-7. Stance is too narrow.

Figure 1-8. Stance is too wide.

Punch begins with the correct position of hands. The down hand should be slightly inside the staggered knee and directly below his eyes. The little finger of the down hand is inside his big toe. The up hand should be cocked at his wrist and the forearm should rest on the top of his knee. The elbow should squeeze the knee of his inside leg to aid in keeping his weight on the arches. No weight should be on his hand. Maintaining this proper hand position leads to an advantage at the line.

The head is up but not back. The eyes scan the defense, observing not only what is in front of the player, but everything around him. Players can be instructed to look out of the "bottoms" of their eyes. It is not necessary to see the opponents' faces, but at least their lower bodies should be visible.

Figure 1-9. Incorrect head position—the head and eyes are down. The player cannot see.

Figure 1-10. Incorrect head position—the head is too high, which forces the player's rear end to drop.

Coaching Point

The head must be relaxed and forward (Figure 1-11). If the head tilts back, the player's butt is pushed down, and his weight is transferred to the heels.

Figure 1-11. Proper position of the head

To be able to get off on the snap count, a lineman must be able to "load up his toe." By pushing his big toe into the surface, a player achieves weight distribution without tipping off the defenders to the lineman's planned angle of departure.

Coaching Point

Load up the toe: Have the player push his big toe into the ground to achieve weight transfer, thus allowing him to be light on his stepping foot.

Figure 1-12 illustrates the key aspects of a proper stance, including:

- Stagger: Outside foot toe-to-instep or toe-to-heel of inside foot
- Base: Feet are shoulder-width apart
- Weight: On the arches
- Hands: The little finger of the down hand is inside the big toe
- Head: Up, not back
- Eyes: Scan the defense

Shuffle: Side-to-side movement while maintaining a constant base (Figure 1-13)

Figure 1-12. Proper stance

Figure 1-13. Shuffle with a base

Run and Shuffle

An offensive lineman uses skills unique to football. A lineman must be able to run, backpedal, and shuffle in a different manner from any other athlete. In normal running, backpedaling, and shuffling, the object is to cover as much ground as possible. An offensive lineman's goal, however, is to maintain his base. He must never have one foot off the ground any longer than possible. His feet must never be together. Just as it would be impossible to walk into a squat rack and squat anything with feet together, it's impossible to survive on the offensive line with feet together.

Coaching Point

> The same base required in a squat or power clean lift is required on the offensive line.

Run and Backpedal

Four points should be taught to offensive linemen when teaching proper run and backpedal maneuvers (Figure 1-14):

- The player should run by sticking his arches into the ground. Doing so keeps his body weight balanced and off the toes.

- Each stride should measure only six to eight inches to keep the feet as close to the ground as possible allowing linemen to keep two legs on the ground. One leg on the ground creates an unstable base.

- Feet stay close to the ground. The knees are not picked up high; the cleats should brush the top of the grass.

- Arms pump as in normal running

Figure 1-14. Run and backpedal with a base

Backpedal: Running backwards with the same form used to run forward

Coaching Point

Backpedaling is the exact same form as running forward, except that the player cannot see where he is going.

Shuffle

The basic lateral movement on the line of scrimmage must be executed flawlessly. Any movement with one foot must be matched by an equal movement with the other foot to maintain a base. Perfect shuffle technique requires attention to four points:

On the duck: Maintaining a proper and consistent base through a series of moves or through an entire block

- Knees are always bent. Linemen should assume the "sit on the bar stool" stance and maintain the stance.

- Shuffle by reaching with the ankles. The reach step moves sideways four to six inches and lands on the arches while the foot points forward.

- The reach step and the slide step are each four to six inches. The football shuffle differs from the basketball shuffle in which the player's ankles knock together, creating an unstable base. A stable base is inconsequential in basketball but fundamental to the offensive line. The lineman's reach step must match his shuffle step perfectly, preserving the solid base required for a successful block.

- The feet never touch each other. Linemen should maintain their base at all times.

Coaching Point

An offensive lineman cannot play the game with his feet together.

Wave Drill

Leverage: The position which places the offensive lineman between the ball and the defender

Once the lineman knows how to sit on the bar stool and run and shuffle, coaches can conduct a wave drill. In this drill, the linemen move at the coach's direction. The linemen may be required to run forward, run backward, or shuffle left or right at random. The object of the wave drill is for the linemen to demonstrate their ability to change direction on sight, just as they will be required to do in play when the defenders change direction.

Step

Offensive linemen must master the basics of run and shuffle using short, choppy steps and "staying on the duck." Throughout all of these moves, linemen must maintain a proper base. Once linemen demonstrate their ability to perform these moves in wave drills, coaches can move to instruction of the first step of each individual block and the angle of departure.

Angle of Departure

The angle of departure is critical to gaining position on the defender. Strong visualization and understanding of "shooting ducks" help the lineman realize he is blocking a moving target. In every individual block, the first step is less than eight inches. The first player to get his first two steps into the ground and his hands inside usually wins the block. To achieve this goal, the first steps must be short and quick.

**Point of attack:
The hole where
the play will run**

The lineman takes the third step on the angle, which allows him to gain position on the defender. The proper position allows the lineman to gain leverage on the defender in relationship to the point of attack.

Individual Steps

Bucket Step

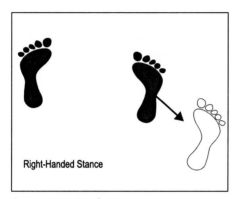

Figure 1-15. Bucket step

A bucket step (Figure 1-15) is a short, quick drop step that allows the lineman to "lose ground to gain ground." The basic bucket step is a six- to eight-inch step that starts with a 45-degree angle. This angle puts the shoulders on a path to block the defender. The lineman's instep rests on the ground. The bucket step has width and depth, which varies based upon the width of the down defender from the offensive lineman. Remember: width *and* depth.

The key aspects of a bucket step are as follows:

- *Type of Step:* Bucket Step
- *Description:* Lose ground to gain ground
- *Coaching Reminder:* Width and depth
- *Pitfall:* Failure to change the width and depth of the step in relationship to the width of the defender results in missing the landmark and the punch.

Coaching Point

> The outside of your player's shoes should look brand new. The insteps should look worn out. Worn insteps indicate correct stepping.

Zone Step

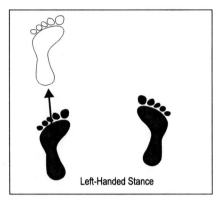

Figure 1-16. Zone step

A zone step (Figure 1-16) is a short, quick over-and-up step that allows a lineman to gain ground on the first step. The basic zone step is a six- to eight-inch step with the instep. The zone step allows the lineman to establish contact with the defender more quickly.

The key aspects of a zone step are as follows:

- *Type of Step:* Zone step
- *Description:* Over and up
- *Coaching Reminder:* Gain ground on first step
- *Pitfall:* Take the angle of the step in the direction of the defender's movement (shooting ducks), and not in the defender's direction prior to the snap.

Up Step

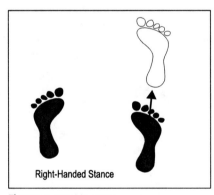

Figure 1-17. Up step

An up step (Figure 1-17) is a short, quick step straight up the field into the defender. This step is primarily used on double team blocks. The basic up step is a six- to eight-inch step that allows the lineman to get into "half" of the defender quickly.

The key aspects of an up step are as follows:

- *Type of Step:* Up step
- *Description:* Double-team block

- *Coaching Reminder:* Gain ground on the first step and initiate contact
- *Pitfall:* The tendency is to step to the edge of the defender and not directly up and into the middle of the defender.

Crossover Step

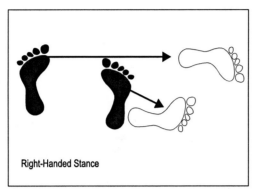

Right-Handed Stance

Figure 1-18. Crossover step

A crossover step (Figure 1-18) is a longer sideways step. The lineman moves over the adjacent lineman and into the defender. If moving right, the left foot crosses the right foot as the right pivots. This crossover allows two adjacent linemen to exchange blocking responsibilities.

The key aspects of a crossover step are as follows:

- *Type of Step:* Crossover step
- *Description:* Longer sideways step to cover as much ground as possible
- *Coaching Reminder:* One foot pivots and the other crosses over at the same time.
- *Pitfall:* This step has to be directly sideways or slightly behind the pivot foot. If the lineman steps into the line of scrimmage he will miss the landmark and therefore miss the cut.

Slide Step

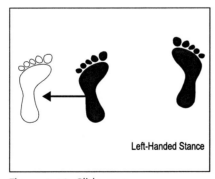

Left-Handed Stance

Figure 1-19. Slide step

A slide step (Figure 1-19) is a short (four- to six-inch), quick step that moves laterally. The sideways slide step allows the lineman to gain inside/outside position on the defender.

The key aspects of a slide step are as follows:

- *Type of Step:* Slide step
- *Description:* Quick lateral step
- *Coaching Reminder:* Gain lateral position
- *Pitfall:* If the step is too long, the lineman's base will be too wide and he will block too much of the defender. This hinders his movement through the block.

Pivot Step

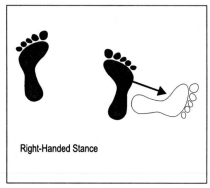

Right-Handed Stance

Figure 1-20. Pivot step

A pivot step (Figure 1-20) is a turn of the foot with the weight on the heel of the foot. The pivot step is used to point the toe in the direction of the block.

The key aspects of a pivot step are as follows:

- *Type of Step:* Pivot step
- *Description:* A turn of the foot
- *Coaching Reminder:* Weight transfer from arch to heel
- *Pitfall:* Many linemen won't point the toe in the direction that they want to go.

Punch

The lineman must know where his hands go on every block. On every punch, the lineman's hands whip off the ground into the defender. Contact with the hands usually happens on the second step. The lineman must try to gain inside hand position on the defender in order to win the block. Inside hand position allows the lineman to have more control over the defender. Coaches should drill players on the following six punches.

Full Bench

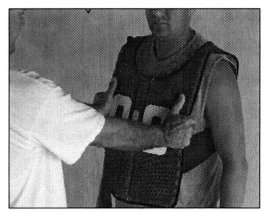

Figure 1-21. Full bench punch

In full bench (Figure 1-21), both hands whip into the defender in an attempt to get maximum control. Full bench is a position of strength in which the player's thumbs are up and his elbows are in close to his body.

Half Bench

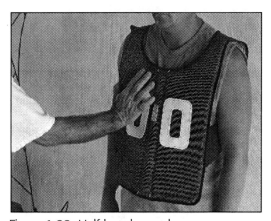

Figure 1-22. Half-bench punch

In half-bench punch (Figure 1-22), the lineman places one hand on the defender. A lineman uses this punch knowing that he will receive help from another lineman. Players use half-bench punch in double-team situations where the lineman works from a down defender to a linebacker.

Flipper

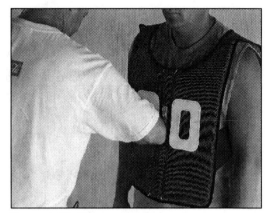

Figure 1-23. Flipper punch

To use the flipper (Figure 1-23), a lineman wads his hands into fists and throws his forearms into the chest of the defender. Both individual and double-team blocks may engage the flipper. Linemen use the flipper in an individual block when attempting to get movement on the defender. As soon as the defender reacts to the block, the lineman may go to a full bench or a rip. He may also leave the defender and move to another defender. Double-team blocks use the flipper to move the down lineman off the line of scrimmage and into a specific linebacker.

Rip

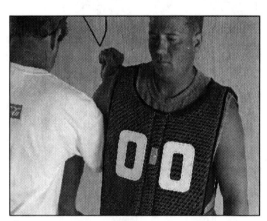

Figure 1-24. Rip punch

In a rip (Figure 1-24), the lineman leads with his fists and blocks with his entire arm, throwing through the defender's armpit. The rip is typically used on a wide play with fast flow.

Reach and Rip

Reach and rip is similar to rip, but the lineman reaches across one player before ripping. For example, the tackle may block the defender by reaching over the guard. The lineman must reach then rip the defender.

Two-Hand Takeover

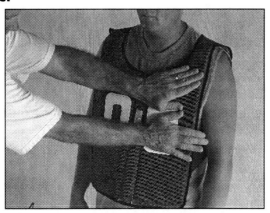

Figure 1-25. Two-hand takeover punch

Double-team blocks use a two-hand takeover (Figure 1-25). In this punch, a lineman throws both hands into the landmark (usually the playside breast) and takes over the down defender. Doing so frees up his blocking partner to go to the linebacker. Unlike the full-bench punch, the lineman leads with both hands thrown into one side of the defender in a two-hand takeover. With this punch, the helmet is not a factor until the defender reacts to the play.

Positions

Linemen have already learned the characteristics of every block: step, landmark, and punch. The length of each step depends upon leverage, point of attack, and position (either inside or outside). Steps give linemen an angle of departure that increases their chances for success. Position is the relationship of the feet and the body to the defender. Perfect blocking position ("fit") allows the player to block the defender effectively through the whistle ("finish"). Perfect position is the fit that leads to the finish.

Position: The relationship of the feet and the body to the defender

Tract is perfect toe-to-toe alignment between an offensive lineman and a defensive player. Linemen should not assume this position; toe-to-toe alignment is never advantageous to a lineman. Instead, it is the starting point from which all other positions derive. The lineman should learn three positions, each with an inside and outside tract, as shown in Figures 1-27 through 1-32.

Position	Inside	Outside
Tract	The offensive lineman's feet are inside the feet of the defensive player.	The offensive lineman's feet are outside the feet of the defensive player.
Midline Tract	The offensive lineman's feet are inside the feet of the defender, and the outside foot is splitting his crotch.	The offensive lineman's feet are outside the feet of the defender, and the inside foot is splitting his crotch.
Foot Tract	The offensive lineman's feet are inside the feet of the defender, and the outside foot is aligned on the defender's inside foot.	The offensive lineman's feet are outside the feet of the defender, and the outside foot is aligned on the defender's outside foot.

Figure 1-26. Tract series

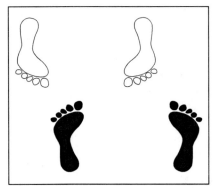

Figure 1-27. Outside tract

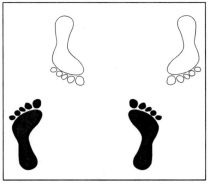

Figure 1-28. Inside tract

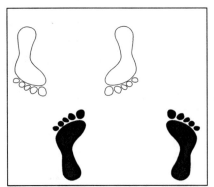

Figure 1-29. Outside midline tract

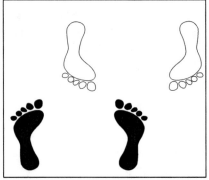

Figure 1-30. Inside midline tract

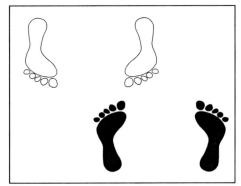

Figure 1-31. Outside foot tract

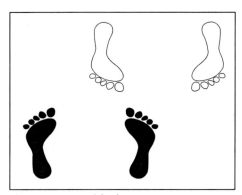

Figure 1-32. Inside foot tract

Block	Outside Tract	Inside Tract	Outside Midline Tract	Inside Midline Tract	Outside Foot Tract	Inside Foot Tract
Base Block	*					
Base Cutoff		*				
Base Stretch			*			
Blunt						*
Bump					*	*
Chip		*				*
Choke		*				
Crossover Lunge					*	*
Funnel and Hinge				*		
Rub	*		*	*		
Scoop	*	*	*		*	
Sift						*
Slide	*	*	*		*	
Slug						*
Tag	*		*	*		
Tug				*		

Figure 1-33. Position chart

Armed with the basics of the offensive line, players are now ready to focus on blocks. The fundamentals of specific blocks will be detailed in Chapter 2. Figure 1-33 indicates the blocks covered in the chapter and the corresponding steps taught in this chapter. For maximum impact on the offensive line, linemen should be able to identify the correct position for each block.

Coach's Clipboard

Four C's
- Confidence
- Consistency
- Concentration
- Cohesiveness

Thought Process
- Who
- When
- Where
- What

Visualization
- See the block
- Shooting ducks
- Defenders will be moving

Blocking Failures
- Mental errors
- Angle of departure
- Missed snap count
- Loafing
- Loss of base
- No punch
- Lack of finish

Unique Skills of Offensive Linemen
- Run
- Shuffle
- Wave drill
- Sit on the bar stool

Stance
- Stagger
- Base
- Arches in the ground
- Light hand
- Eyes up, head relaxed
- Loaded big toe

Blocks
- Step
- Landmark
- Punch

Steps
- Bucket
- Zone
- Up
- Crossover
- Slide
- Pivot

Positions
- Inside tract
- Outside tract
- Inside midline tract
- Outside midline tract
- Inside-foot tract
- Outside-foot tract

RUN BLOCKS

Jonathan Daniel/Getty Images

Chapter Two

Once linemen have a solid grasp of the fundamentals of step, landmark, and punch, the coaching focus expands to emphasize the physical components of offensive play. In this chapter, linemen build the repertoire of the physical and mental aspects of the offensive game with individual blocks and two- and three-man combination blocks. Coaching expands on technique and teaches the proper position of the feet, head, and hands in each block (emphasizing the "where" thought on every snap). The focus on technique continues to highlight three of the blocking failures from Chapter 1: angle of departure, loss of base, and no punch.

Players will learn four basic individual blocks:

- Base
- Base stretch
- Base cutoff (inside play)
- Base cutoff (outside play)

These blocks shape the foundation of the two-man and (later) three-man combos. When teaching these blocks, coaches should emphasize the importance of correct step, landmark, and punch, as well as the mechanics of each block.

On every block, the lineman will need to determine the correct first step (bucket, slide, etc.). The coach may adjust the first step of any block to match his beliefs or coaching philosophy, and the ability of the player. Regardless of which first step the coach teaches, players must come off the ball with a right- or left-foot lead. This fundamental move, called "loading up the toe," should be emphasized because the first step makes a successful block possible. Loading up the toe makes a lineman light on his foot allowing him to take a stance that looks the same—whether setting up a pass or run play. Loading up his toe allows a lineman to avoid tipping off the defenders.

When teaching a proper base block, the coach may want to begin with a bucket step and then move to a zone step. Regardless of which step is first, the player loads his toe. Moving to the right, the player uses a right-foot lead (loading up his left big toe). Moving left, the player uses a left-foot lead (loading up his right big toe).

The landmarks are adjusted on each block depending upon the point of attack and the play's tempo (slow or fast flow). When considering point of attack, the lineman must recognize that the closer he is to the point of attack, the more of the defender he must cover. A lineman who is close to the point of attack must position himself

Coaching Point

The amount of time that it takes the defense to react to the play determines if a play is fast flow or slow flow. A toss sweep is a fast-flow play because the defense sees the ball in the air and reacts to the path of the ballcarrier. A draw is a slow-flow play because the defense reads pass first and then sees a late handoff to the ballcarrier.

closer to the midline of the defender. This same adjustment is made for a faster flow play. The faster the flow of the play, the farther the landmark moves from the midline of the defender's body.

About the Blocks

Each blocking page indicates when the block should be utilized, the lineman's position, first and second step, landmark (helmet placement), punch (arms), and mechanics. The Coach's Whistle sections, included throughout the blocking section, feature tips for successful blocks and pitfalls leading to common mistakes encountered in coaching and performing the blocks.

Note that in the step descriptions, the word "outside" is used to describe the foot that is farthest from the point of attack. For example, a left tackle's outside foot is his left foot if the point of attack is to his right.

Base Block (Figure 2-1)

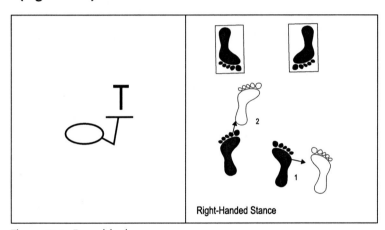

Right-Handed Stance

Figure 2-1. Base block

Description: Use this block on an inside run by a covered lineman with no help from the backside lineman and no linebacker responsibility.

Position: Outside tract

First Step: Bucket/zone with outside foot

Second Step: A short and quick step with the inside foot, stepping into the shoe of the defender, which is the direction of the step and not the length of the step

Landmark: Playside breast

Punch: Full bench

Mechanics: The helmet should be placed on the playside breast (landmark), and the fist and arms should whip into the defender's armpits (punch). The offensive lineman

(OL) applies most of his strength to the hand nearest the point of attack, and uses short, choppy steps (stays on the duck) with a wide base. The lineman must have patience waiting for the defender to tell the offensive lineman what he is doing. Coach the linemen to finish the block, pushing one more time at the whistle.

Coach's Whistle:

- Players who miss the angle will miss the block. Note whether the bucket step turned the shoulders on an angle to block the defender. If the lineman doesn't turn on the angle, he'll miss the landmark, hitting the inside breast due to his stretching.

- The tendency on the second step is to move sideways rather than up into the defender. If the defender moves outside, the lineman moves inside. Shoulders that turn to the boundary lose the angle needed to make the block.

- If the helmet goes to the playside breast, the defender is forced to play his gap, which helps define the hole for the running back.

- The first two steps must be in the ground before contact.

- When the offensive lineman hits his landmark, the defender is forced to play his assigned gap creating the running lanes. Covering the correct half of the defender keeps all run lanes open.

DEFENSIVE ID

Defensive alignments are indicated by numbering techniques:

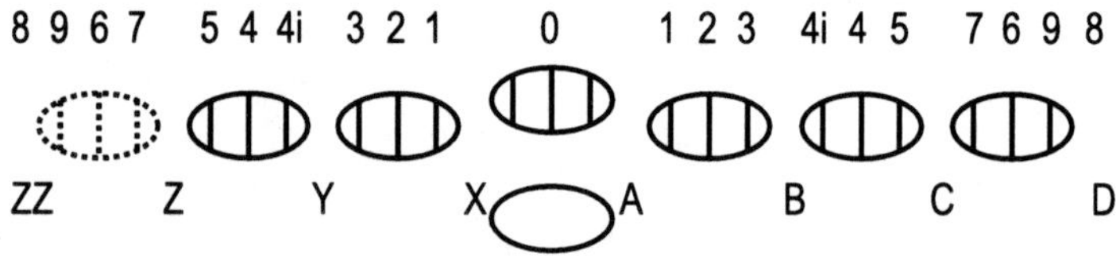

8 9 6 7   5 4 4i   3 2 1   0   1 2 3   4i 4 5   7 6 9 8

ZZ   Z   Y   X   A   B   C   D

Defensive Alignment Terms:
1-2-3 Technique—A defender aligned over the offensive guard
4-4i-5 Technique—A defender aligned over the offensive tackle
6-7-9 Technique—A defender aligned over the tight end or ghost TE
8 Technique—A defender aligned outside the TE
Shade Technique—Nose aligned on the center, but not head-up
A Gap—Area between center and guard (TE side)
B Gap—Area between guard and tackle (TE side)
C Gap—Area between tackle and TE (TE side)
D Gap—Area outside TE (TE side)
X Gap—Area between center and guard (open side, no TE)
Y Gap—Area between guard and tackle (open side)
Z Gap—Area between tackle and TE (open side)
ZZ Gap—Area outside weakside TE

Figure 2-2. Defensive identification (alignment, technique and gap responsibility)

Base Stretch (Figure 2-3)

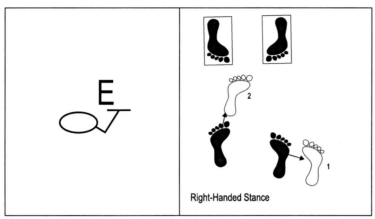

Figure 2-3. Base stretch

Description: This block is the same as the base block, but the point of attack is wider. Base stretch is used by a covered lineman on an outside run with no help from the backside lineman and no linebacker responsibility.

Position: Outside midline tract

First Step: Bucket/zone with outside foot

Second Step: A short, quick step with the inside foot to the crotch of the defender, which is the direction of the step, and not the length of the step

Landmark: Playside armpit

Punch: Full bench

Mechanics: The helmet should be placed on the playside armpit (landmark). The outside hand is on the shoulder and the inside hand is on the chest (punch). The offensive lineman should be strongest with the hand nearest the point of attack. The offensive lineman must use short, choppy steps (stays on the duck) with a wide base. He must have patience, waiting until the defender communicates his intent. Once the defender commits either inside or outside, the offensive lineman defines the hole by finishing the block.

Coach's Whistle:

- Did the bucket step turn the shoulders on an angle to block the defender? If the offensive lineman doesn't turn on the angle, he'll miss the landmark.

- The tendency on the second step is to step too long, which turns the shoulders to the sideline and releases the defender to the outside. The offensive lineman has not defined the hole and forces the back to make an early cut.

- If the helmet goes to the armpit, the defender is forced to work wider, helping the play.

- If the defender stretches and will not let the lineman gain outside leverage, at some point, the lineman's shoulders turn parallel to the boundary. When this parallel turn happens, the offensive lineman pushes the defender with the inside hand and forces him to the boundary. This move tells the ballcarrier to make his cut inside the block. The hole has been defined inside.

- Covering the correct half of the defender keeps all run lanes open.

Funnel and Hinge (Figure 2-4)

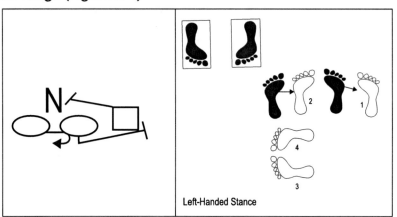

Figure 2-4. Funnel and hinge

Description: A block favored by the Washington Redskins, funnel and hinge is used by a backside tackle to protect the two backside gaps when the offense runs gap/power schemes. The funnel and hinge is used in misdirection plays only.

Position: Inside midline tract

First Step: Power with the inside foot (1-set)

Second Step: A slide step that continues 1-set to protect inside gap

Landmark: Shoulder

Punch: Half bench

Mechanics: The offensive lineman pre-reads the inside down defender on his guard or center and 1-sets down the line of scrimmage to the down defender. If the defender is a nose, the offensive lineman sees the linebacker to the defensive end and prevents a run through blitzer. If the defense has no blitzer, the offensive lineman pivots and looks for a trailing defender forcing him upfield. If the defender is a 3 technique, the offensive lineman reads the leg of the 3 technique. If he is moving toward the offensive lineman, the offensive lineman stays on him. If the 3 technique is moving away from the offensive lineman, the offensive lineman sees the linebacker to the defensive end and prevents a run through blitzer.

Coach's Whistle:

- Shortening the 1-set and pivoting too early (instead of reading the defense) compromises the block.

- The offensive lineman must protect the inside gap run-through. If any threat is present, the offensive lineman forgets the 1-set and cuts the existing threat in the gap. The inside gaps must be protected because penetration will kill the play.

Crossover Lunge (Figure 2-5)

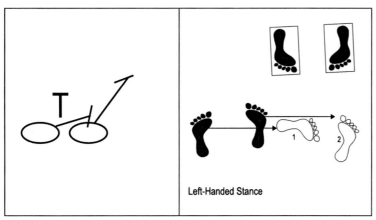

Figure 2-5. Crossover lunge

Description: Crossover lunge cuts the inside down defender who covers the adjacent offensive lineman. This block is mainly used on the backside and on the goal line.

Position: Inside midline tract

First Step: Crossover with outside foot

Second Step: The inside foot should pivot at the same time as the crossover is occurring

Landmark: Playside leg

Punch: None

Mechanics: The offensive lineman takes the first step with the backside foot crossing over (step) and aiming at the defender's playside knee. The offensive lineman makes contact with the shoulder, throwing his backside arm past the playside hip of the defender. If the offensive lineman does not cut the defender upon contact, he should roll and tie him up. (Roll his body into the defender attempting to take him down. Once he's down, the offensive lineman tangles his body up with the defender's to keep him down.) The offensive lineman pins the defender to the ground.

Coach's Whistle:

- Stepping into the line of scrimmage instead of targeting the defender's playside leg will put the lineman behind the defender and not in front. The crossover step must be straight through or slightly behind the lineman's inside foot. If the crossover step is into the line of scrimmage, the offensive lineman's body penetrates the line colliding with the defender's body. Instead, the offensive lineman should cross the defender's playside knee (Figure 2-6).

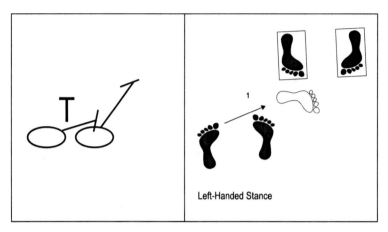

Figure 2-6. The lineman steps into the line of scrimmage instead of taking a lateral step.

- The offensive lineman must get his body into the air and cover as much ground as possible because the defender will be running away from the block (shooting ducks).
- The down defender reads the lineman in front of him and reacts to his release. Keeping low pads will keep the lineman's knee high on the defender. This low pad level will prevent the defender from knocking the lineman off the block with his upper body.

Sift (Figure 2-7)

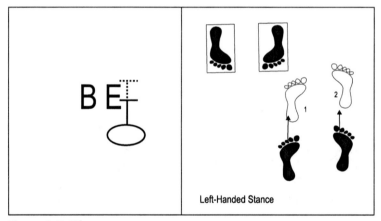

Figure 2-7. Sift

Description: Used by the backside tackle away from the point of attack (tackle versus down lineman and outside linebacker).

Position: Inside-foot tract

First Step: Up with outside foot

Second Step: Up with inside foot. The tighter the defender, the shorter the step. The inside foot needs to be behind the outside foot on contact.

Landmark: Near number

Punch: Flipper

Mechanics: Before the snap, the offensive lineman reads the down defender for alignment. If he's facing a 4 technique with an outside linebacker, the offensive lineman rips through the inside number of the down defender. If the down defender engages, the offensive lineman stays with him. (The lineman feels the pressure of the down defender against his hip or side. The more pressure the lineman feels, the more he stays with the defender and blocks.) If the down defender works upfield or loosens, the offensive lineman works a path upfield and blocks the linebacker. If facing a 5 technique, the offensive lineman rips the inside number of the down defender and works a path to block the linebacker.

Coach's Whistle

- If the defender is tight, the lineman must step through the midline of the defender and not step around. The step moves through the defender's crotch to get contact.

- The offensive lineman should not work upfield too fast letting the defender react first to the flow of the play. The offensive lineman stays on the duck.

Choke (Figure 2-8)

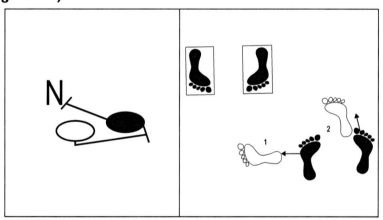

Figure 2-8. Choke

Description: This block is only used with a gap or power scheme (slow-flow) play. The center uses choke to block back to a down defender over the pulling guard.

Position: Inside tract

First Step: Pivot with the backside foot

Second Step: A zone step that hangs in the air until the defender reacts to a pulling guard (like a dog peeing on a fire hydrant).

Landmark: If nose guard is a helmet reader, near neck. If nose guard is a penetrator, ear hole

Helmet reader: A defender who reads the release of the lineman.

Penetrator: A defender who attacks his assigned gap.

The defense is coached to play as penetrators or helmet readers. Viewing game film helps determine if the defender is a helmet reader or a penetrator.

Penetrator: A defender who attacks his assigned gap

Punch: Full bench, but the center must put his inside hand on the defender's hip

Mechanics: The offensive lineman steps down the line of scrimmage and flattens the down defender assuming penetration by the defender. The offensive lineman stops the penetrating defender so that he does not get in the path of a pulling guard. The offensive lineman adjusts his angle to a defender that tries to fight across his face.

Coaching Point

A defender has only two options: penetrate or fight across your face.

Coach's Whistle:

- Penetration will hurt the play more than a defender pursuing down the line of scrimmage. The offensive lineman should not allow the defender penetration.

- Correct landmark is critical to getting the play started. Game plan the landmark based on how the defender plays a pulling guard in game films. Run the block according to previous knowledge of the defenders, and adjust after confirmation during the game. If unsure of the defender's tendency, the offensive lineman aims for the ear hole of his helmet (penetrator) and then adjusts during the game.

Reverse Hip (Figure 2-9)

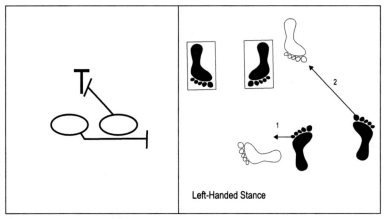

Figure 2-9. Reverse hip

Description: Used when a lineman needs to block away from the point of attack to a down defender over a pulling lineman. This play adds an aggravation factor to the defense. Because it's ugly, it is seldom used, but it is nice for a coach to have in his arsenal.

First Step: Pivot with inside foot

Position: Outside foot tract

Second Step: A leg whip that turns the body 180 degrees and cuts the defender's leg out from under him.

Landmark: Between the legs

Punch: None

Mechanics: The offensive lineman steps down the line of scrimmage and gets his head between the defender's legs and keeps it up. The offensive lineman must make contact, and then whip his legs around.

Coach's Whistle:

- Linemen who throw the body too early without making contact with the head and shoulders lose the block.

- Reverse hip is used as a change up on a down defender to "get into his head." Defenders hate blocks around their knees.

Backside Cutoff Outside Play (Figure 2-10)

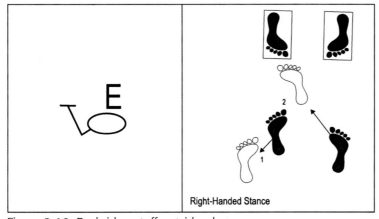

Figure 2-10. Backside cutoff outside play

Description: This block is used by a covered lineman on the backside of an outside play with no help from the backside lineman. All two-man combos on the backside are variations of a backside cutoff.

Position: Inside-foot tract

First Step: Bucket with inside foot

Second Step: Zone with outside foot. The lineman matches his far foot to the defender's far foot. This step is a short and quick step with the outside foot to the defender's inside foot, which is the direction of his step and not the length of his step.

Landmark: Playside armpit

Punch: Rip

Mechanics: The offensive lineman takes a bucket step thinking, "Deeper and wider." The second step is the lineman's far foot to the defender's far foot. The hat should be placed on the playside armpit (landmark). The rip (punch) should be thrown through the armpit of the defender. The offensive lineman stays up and runs the defender into the next pile. If he loses the defender, he uses a speed turn to pin him.

Coaching Point

A speed turn is an efficient maneuver that runs counter to instinct for some players. The turn involves no pivot. Instead, the lineman turns away from the defender briefly losing sight of the defender but gaining the advantage with speed.

Coach's Whistle:

- Did the bucket step turn the shoulders on an angle to block the defender?

- The tendency on the second step is to step around and not through the defender. The offensive lineman must make contact. His objective is to keep the block as big as possible.

- The bucket step is deeper and wider because the point of attack is wider.

- The offensive lineman should stay on the duck and hold his ground. If the defender runs, the offensive lineman turns the block into a crossover lunge and cuts him.

- The rip could turn into a full bench due to the reaction of the defender. If the defender reacts across the face of the offensive lineman, punch turns to full bench. If the defender goes behind the offensive lineman, the offensive lineman uses a speed turn to reach him.

Backside Cutoff Inside Play (Figure 2-11)

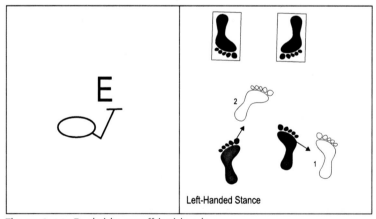

Figure 2-11. Backside cutoff inside play

Description: This block is used by a covered lineman on the backside of an inside play with no help from a backside lineman. All two-man combos on the backside are variations of a backside cutoff.

Position: Inside midline tract

First Step: Bucket with inside foot

Second Step: Zone with outside foot. The lineman matches his far foot to the defender's far foot. This step is a short and quick step with the outside foot to the defenders inside foot, which is the direction of the step, not the length of the step. Contact with the flipper should be made on this step.

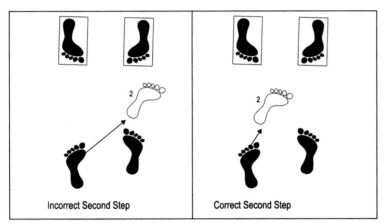

Figure 2-12. Correct step and poor step, the lineman steps around the down defender.

Landmark: Playside breast

Punch: Flipper

Mechanics: The hat should be placed on the playside breast (landmark). The flipper (punch) should be thrown into the chest of the defender. The offensive lineman must use short, choppy steps (stay on the duck) with a wide base, trying to push his hips through the defender's hips. The offensive lineman must have patience and wait for the defender to tell him what he is doing. If the offensive lineman loses the defender, he uses a butt block (blocking with his butt and lower body to screen the defender from the ball) to pin the defender.

Coach's Whistle:

- Did the bucket step turn the shoulders on an angle to block the defender? Have the player visualize the angle and the block.
- The tendency on the second step is to step around and not through the defender.
- The bucket step is deeper and wider as the defender's alignment gets tighter.
- The bucket step is deeper and wider due to the speed of the defender. The offensive lineman is shooting ducks and steps into the defender's path.
- Once the defender reacts, the punch will go from the flipper to a full bench or rip.
- The offensive lineman stays on the duck and holds his ground. He keeps the backside "big," and the cutback lanes open.

Two-Man Combos

The two-man combo block section provides the steps for the covered lineman and the uncovered lineman. In most of these blocks, the down defender has three options: he can either hang (stay on the lineman), slant (move inside), or stretch (read the lineman's hat and work outside or widen). The lineman can read the defender's leg to determine which option the defender will choose. Each blocking page covers these options and defines the mechanics for the covered lineman and the uncovered lineman.

Most of the combo blocks covered in this section are variations of the following individual blocks:

- Base
- Base stretch
- Backside cutoff inside play
- Backside cutoff outside play

Scoop: Covered Lineman (Figure 2-13)

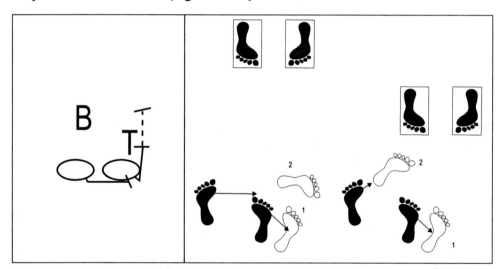

Figure 2-13. Scoop: covered lineman

Description: This block is used in three situations: when the linebacker is in a cheat position (playside), when the linebacker is a fast-flow player, or when running outside plays. The covered lineman will execute a base stretch block with inside help from the adjacent lineman.

Position: Outside midline tract

First Step: Bucket with outside foot

Second Step: A short, quick step with the inside foot to the crotch of the defender, which is the direction of his step not the length of his step.

Landmark: Playside armpit

Punch: Full bench

Mechanics: Use a base stretch block, but be ready to rip through the defender and go to the linebacker.

- If the defender stretches (reads the offensive lineman's helmet), then the offensive lineman base stretches and thinks, "Stay on defender with no help."
- If the down defender hangs, then the offensive lineman base stretches and stays ready for his partner to rip him out taking the path to block the linebacker.
- If the down defender slants, then the offensive lineman stays on the path to block the linebacker.

Coach's Whistle:

- This block is a base stretch; do not allow the offensive lineman to step around the down defender. The offensive lineman should always block the line of scrimmage first.
- The offensive lineman gets on a path in the direction of the linebacker's movement, not his current position (shooting ducks).
- The offensive lineman should never full bench a linebacker on a wide play; he should rip or cut him instead.

Scoop: Uncovered Lineman (Figure 2-14)

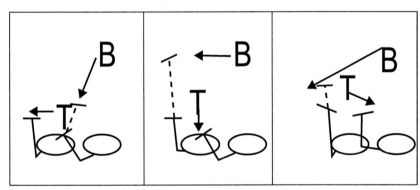

Figure 2-14. Scoop blocking versus defensive reaction

Position: Outside foot tract

First Step: Bucket with outside foot

Second Step: Crossover with inside foot

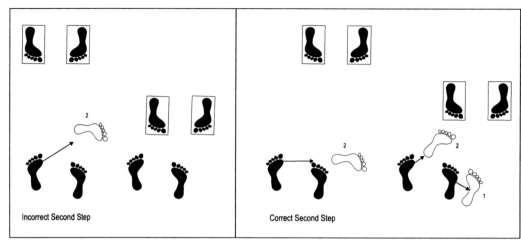

Figure 2-15. Correct second step and poor second step; the second step is into the line of scrimmage and not a crossover lateral step.

Landmark: Playside armpit

Punch: Reach and rip

Mechanics: As the offensive lineman crosses over and turns his body to the sideline, he reads the inside leg of the down defender for three steps.

- If the leg comes toward the offensive lineman, the offensive lineman rips the defender's far armpit and takes over the down lineman allowing his partner to go to the linebacker.

- If the leg stays, then the offensive lineman rips the defender's far armpit and takes over the down lineman. He forces his partner off the block of the linebacker.

- If the leg goes away, then the offensive lineman stays on the path for three steps, and then puts his eyes on the linebacker. The offensive lineman stays on a cutoff path to the linebacker. When he gets close enough, the offensive lineman cuts or rips the linebacker's playside armpit or knee.

Coach's Whistle:

- If the crossover step is too flat into the line of scrimmage, the lineman cannot reach the far armpit. If the defender slants inside, he will hit the lineman on his playside shoulder and destroy the block.

- The lineman must read the down defender's inside leg for three steps. Doing so will keep the lineman on his path to blocking either the down defender or the linebacker.

- The offensive lineman never full benches a linebacker on wide plays.

Slip: Covered Lineman (Figure 2-16)

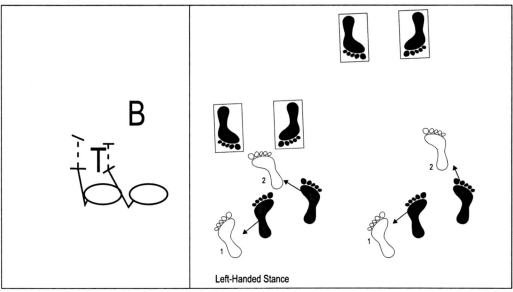

Figure 2-16. Slip: covered lineman

Description: A combination block used to double-team a down defensive lineman from the line of scrimmage to a linebacker. The covered lineman executes a base block with inside help from the adjacent lineman.

Position: Outside tract

First Step: Bucket with outside foot

Second Step: A short, quick step with the inside foot, stepping in the shoe of the defender. Player should match the direction of his step not the length of his step.

Landmark: Playside breast

Punch: Full bench

Mechanics: Use a base block with inside help from the inside lineman.

- If defender stretches, then the offensive lineman base blocks thinking, "Stay on defender with no help."

- If defender hangs, then the offensive lineman base blocks with half bench help from the inside lineman. The offensive lineman stays on double-team until the linebacker commits.

- If defender slants inside, then the offensive lineman half benches the defensive linebacker with inside help. He looks for a quick linebacker over the top. When the linebacker shows up outside, the offensive lineman comes off the down defender and uses full bench technique to block the linebacker.

Coach's Whistle:

- This block is a base block. The offensive lineman blocks the line of scrimmage first and does not step around the down defender.
- The offensive lineman moves in the direction the linebacker's reaction, not his present position (shooting ducks).
- The offensive lineman must have more patience than the linebacker. The offensive lineman continues to double-team until the linebacker commits.

Coaching Points

A full bench never goes to "no hands." If the down defender reacts so that the offensive lineman cannot use both hands, the lineman must get one hand on the defender to protect his partner.

When double-teaming the line of scrimmage, if the down defender steps to the covered lineman, the covered lineman full benches, and the uncovered lineman half benches. If the down defender slants to the uncovered lineman, the covered lineman half benches, and the uncovered lineman full benches.

Slip: Uncovered Lineman (Figure 2-17)

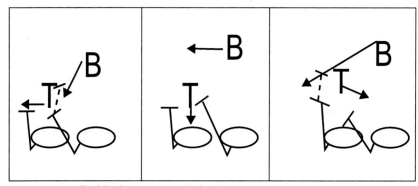

Figure 2-17. Slip blocking versus defensive reaction

Position: Outside tract

First Step: Bucket with outside foot

Second Step: Zone with inside foot into the shoe of the linebacker. This step changes based on the reaction and path of the linebacker to the football.

Landmark: Playside breast

Punch: Half bench

Mechanics: As the lineman steps into the shoe of the linebacker (LB), he feels for the down defender with his outside hand (half bench).

- If the linebacker comes toward the OL and the down defender stretches, then the offensive lineman stays on the duck and blocks the linebacker with a full bench technique.

- If the linebacker stacks behind a down lineman, then the offensive lineman stays on the double team with a half bench punch and reads the linebacker. The offensive lineman stays on double team until the linebacker forces the offensive lineman to block him.

- If the linebacker runs to outside gap, then the offensive lineman takes over the down lineman and base blocks him with a full bench punch.

Coach's Whistle:

- The lineman doesn't read the path of the linebacker.

- The offensive lineman must be able to focus on one thing but see other things. Coaches can teach this technique as simultaneously using "bright lights" (seeing the backfield action and reading the reaction of the linebacker) and "dim lights" (feeling the down defender with the outside hand and peripheral vision).

- The lineman must stay on the duck to the linebacker and not rush the block. The offensive lineman does not want to block the linebacker before the ball enters the line of scrimmage.

Tag: Covered Lineman (Figure 2-18)

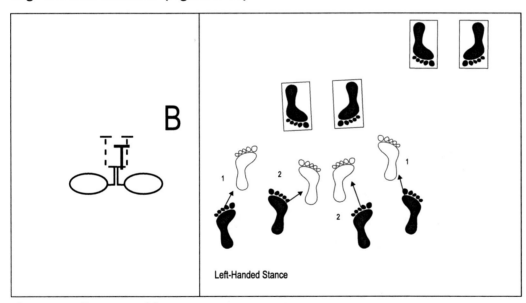

Figure 2-18. Tag: covered lineman

Description: This block is used to double-team a down defender on the line of scrimmage into a designated linebacker. The lineman must move the down defender off the line of scrimmage

Position: Inside midline tract

First Step: If the defender is tight, up step with the outside foot; if defender is loose, zone step with the outside foot. As this step is made, contact should be made with the flipper. The flipper and the foot have to work together; a lineman cannot step with his right foot and throw his left flipper, and vice versa.

Second Step: Up with the outside foot

Landmark: Near number

Punch: Flipper

Mechanics: Use flipper double-team punch. When movement starts, continue pushing with a half-bench punch. Keep eyes on the linebacker.

- If the linebacker stays inside, then the offensive lineman pushes with half bench, comes off the block and blocks the linebacker with a full bench punch.

- If the linebacker stays deep, then the offensive lineman stays on double-team and blocks the linebacker by pushing the defender off the line of scrimmage into the linebacker.

- If the linebacker runs over the top, then the offensive lineman takes over the block on the down defender with a full bench punch.

Coach's Whistle:

- The lineman must get "his half" of the down defender and not step to one side. The lineman should avoid being on the edge.

- As movement on the down defender starts, punch changes from flipper to hand. The offensive lineman continues pushing, keeping his eyes on the linebacker.

- The lineman must be alert for a quick run-through linebacker.

Offensive linemen must be able to focus on one thing but see other things.

Tag: Uncovered Lineman (Figure 2-19)

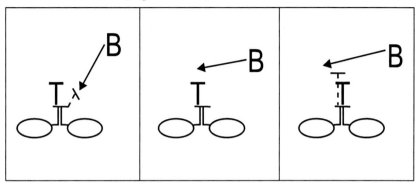

Figure 2-19 Tag blocking versus defensive reaction

Position: Outside midline tract

First Step: If the down defender is loose, up step with the inside foot. If the down defender is tight, slide step with the inside foot.

Second Step: Zone with the outside foot to close the distance between the two linemen. The third step is an up step with the inside foot. As the third step hits the ground, contact should be made with the flipper. The flipper and the foot have to work together.

Landmark: Near number

Punch: Flipper

Mechanics: As the third step hits the ground and contact is made with the flipper, the lineman should be hip-to-hip and shoulder-to-shoulder. As movement starts, the lineman should change his punch from flipper to hand and continue pushing with a half bench. The offensive lineman stays on the double-team with his eyes on the linebacker.

- If the linebacker stays inside, then the offensive lineman takes over the block on the down defender with a full bench punch.
- If the linebacker stays deep, then the offensive lineman stays on the double-team and blocks the linebacker with the defender.
- If the linebacker runs over the top, then the offensive lineman pushes with half bench and comes off the block and blocks the linebacker with full bench punch.

Coach's Whistle:

- The linemen must be hip-to-hip and shoulder-to-shoulder. If this is not accomplished, either the down defender will split the double-team or there will be no movement off the line of scrimmage and the linemen will be working against each other.

Tug: Covered and Uncovered (Figure 2-20)

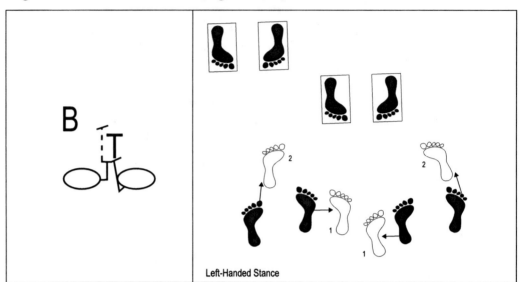

Left-Handed Stance

Figure 2-20. Tug: covered and uncovered

Description: Use tug in place of a tag block when a covered lineman needs to come off the down defender quicker in order to reach the linebacker.

Mechanics: As movement starts, the lineman must change punch from flipper to half bench keeping his eyes on the linebacker. As the lineman comes off the down defender, he pushes the shoulder one more time.

- The *covered lineman* will execute a tag block, knowing his partner is taking over the block and not double-teaming.

- The *uncovered lineman* will execute a base block but will have flipper and inside midline tract help from the covered lineman The offensive lineman should try only to get movement and control of the defender instead of trying to turn him.

Coach's Whistle:

- The covered lineman must block the line of scrimmage first, and then push off to the linebacker.

- The tendency is for the lineman to enter the block behind the partner and turn the defender. Instead, the uncovered lineman must enter the block at a power angle to base block and get movement.

Chip: Covered Lineman (Figure 2-21)

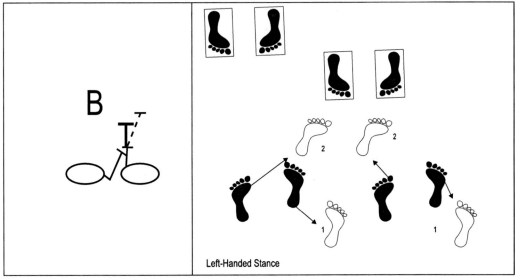

Figure 2-21. Chip: covered lineman

Description: Use chip on the backside of an inside running play to keep the backside running lanes open.

Position: Inside-foot tract

First Step: Bucket with the inside foot

Second Step: Zone with the outside foot

Landmark: Playside shoulder

Punch: Flipper

Mechanics: The covered lineman executes a base cutoff block (inside play) with outside help from an adjacent lineman.

- If the linebacker stays outside, then the offensive lineman takes over the block with a full bench punch.
- If the linebacker hangs, then the offensive lineman stays on double-team and blocks the defender into the linebacker.
- If the linebacker runs over the top, then the offensive lineman pushes the shoulder of the defender and blocks the linebacker with a full bench punch.

Coach's Whistle:

- This block is a double-team block; there must be movement off the line of scrimmage. The lineman must have patience and wait until the linebacker commits to a running lane.
- The offensive lineman should be as physical as possible with one hand.

Chip: Uncovered Lineman (Figure 2-22)

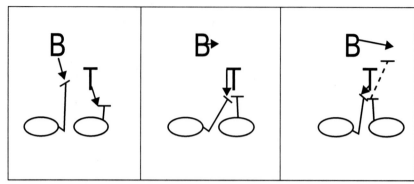

Figure 2-22. Chip blocking versus defensive reaction

Position: Inside-foot tract

First Step: Bucket with inside foot

Second Step: Zone with outside foot

Landmark: Playside armpit

Punch: Two-hand takeover

Mechanics: The uncovered lineman reads the inside leg of the defender.

- If the leg moves away from offensive lineman, then the offensive lineman snaps his hips and blocks the linebacker.
- If the leg comes toward offensive lineman, then the offensive lineman sticks his helmet and both hands into the playside armpit and propels his partner off the double-team to the linebacker.

Coaching Point

The center must keep his face out of the block while pushing on the defender and maintaining eye contact with the middle linebacker.

Collision course: The shortest distance to the down defender

Coach's Whistle:

- The tendency is for the lineman to enter behind the other lineman in a rip alignment. Instead the lineman should enter the block through the chest to the armpit (collision course).

Slug: Covered Lineman (Figure 2-23)

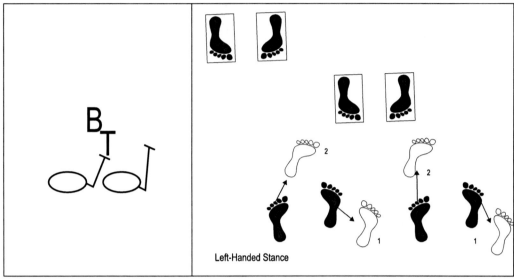

Figure 2-23. Slug: covered lineman

Description: Used on the backside of a running play when a linebacker moves to the playside alignment or the down defender is in a loose alignment.

Position: Inside-foot tract

First Step: Bucket with inside foot

Second Step: Zone with outside foot

Landmark: Near armpit

Punch: Half bench

Mechanics: Bucket step and punch the defender with the inside hand. This bucket step puts the lineman on a path to block the linebacker (visualize angles/shooting ducks).

- If down defender attacks, then the offensive lineman pushes with his inside hand while staying on the duck and staying on a path to the linebacker.

- If down defender runs around the block, then the offensive lineman stays on the duck and on a path to block the linebacker.

Coach's Whistle:

- The linebacker moves to the playside and the lineman must visualize what angle leads to blocking the linebacker.

- Until the backside lineman takes over the block, the covered lineman has the down defender with one hand. Because he is one-on-one, the covered lineman will strain when he first throws the flipper.

Slug: Uncovered Lineman

Position: Inside-foot tract

First Step: Bucket with inside foot

Second Step: Zone with outside foot

Landmark: Playside armpit

Punch: Two-hand takeover

Mechanics: This block is a takeover block and not a read (double-team) block because of the alignment of the defense and/or the speed of the linebacker. In this block, the lineman doesn't read legs. Instead, he exchanges responsibilities because of the defense's alignment. This block is a physical block.

Coach's Whistle:

- The tendency is to enter behind the other lineman in a rip alignment. Instead, the lineman should enter the block through the chest to the armpit (collision course).

Chris Graythen/Getty Images

In the slug block, the lineman doesn't read legs; instead, he exchanges responsibilities because of the defense's alignment.

I'm Gone: Covered Lineman (Figure 2-24)

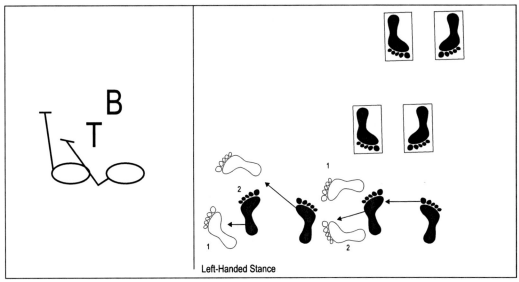

Figure 2-24. I'm gone: covered lineman

Description: This block is used on the backside of a wide running play, or when the linebacker is running and the lineman needs to cut off the linebacker.

Position: Inside-foot tract

First Step: Zone with inside foot

Second Step: Far step with outside foot

Mechanics: Come out running and get on an angle (visualize/shooting ducks) to cut or rip the linebacker.

Coach's Whistle:

- The offensive lineman should stay on the angle and not turn back to the linebacker.
- The offensive lineman "steps on the linebacker's toes" before throwing his body into the block. Doing so puts the lineman close enough to get his shoulders across the defender's playside knee, allowing for a successful block.

Coaching Point

Before attempting to throw his body into the block, the lineman must be close enough to get his shoulder across the playside knee of the linebacker.

I'm Gone: Uncovered Lineman

Mechanics: Execute a crossover lunge.

Rub: Covered Lineman (Figure 2-25)

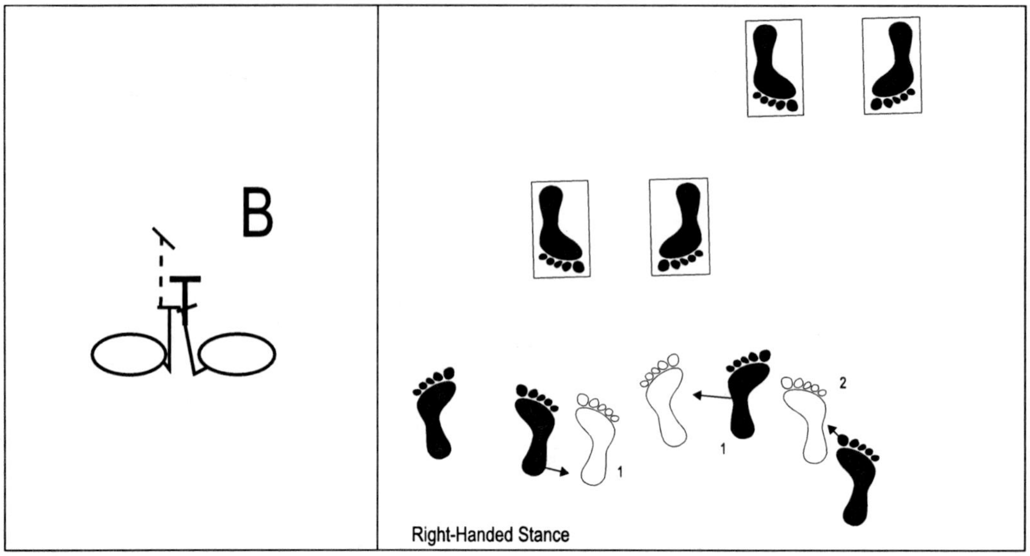

Right-Handed Stance

Figure 2-25. Rub: covered lineman

Description: This block is used on draw plays to show pass and to double-team the line of scrimmage while working slowly toward the linebacker.

Position: Inside midline tract

First Step: 2-set

Second Step: None until down defender reacts

Mechanics: The covered lineman will show pass and wait on a reaction from the down defender. The offensive lineman must stay patient until the defender reacts.

- If the defender reads the pass and attacks, then the offensive lineman steers him up the field and blocks him out of the cylinder

- If the defender reads the pass and attacks the offensive lineman's partner, then the offensive lineman pushes him onto his partner and insures the block. He reads the linebacker and stays under control and on the duck.

- If the defender reads run and hangs, then the offensive lineman double-teams the down defender off the line of scrimmage. He reads the linebacker. If he comes toward the offensive lineman, the offensive lineman blocks with full bench. If he goes over the top, the offensive lineman takes over the down defender.

Coach's Whistle:

- If the lineman doesn't give the down defender a soft shoulder to rush, he will dictate the rush lane. Once the down defender has chosen a rush lane, the lineman must force him out of the cylinder.

- The lineman must secure the line of scrimmage. He must stay patient and let the defense react to the pass drop of the quarterback. If a lineman crosses the line of scrimmage or goes to the linebacker, the linebacker knows the play is not a pass. The offensive lineman should have patience and stay in the pass set, forcing the linebackers to drop as deep as possible. If a lineman shows "run" and goes to the linebacker early, the linebacker reads "run" and does not pass drop.

Rub: Uncovered Lineman (Figure 2-26)

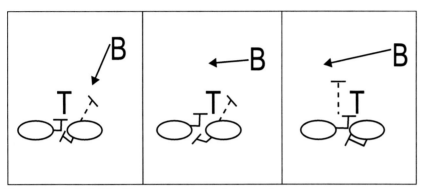

Figure 2-26. Rub blocking versus defensive reaction

Position: Outside midline tract

First step: 1-set

Second step: Slide, continue to 1-set reading the down defender

- If the defender reads the pass and attacks, then the offensive lineman steers him up the field and blocks him out of the cylinder

- If the defender reads the pass and attacks the offensive lineman's partner, the offensive lineman pushes him onto his partner and ensures the block. He reads the linebacker and stays under control and on the duck.

- If the defender reads run and hangs, then the offensive lineman double-teams the down defender off the line of scrimmage and reads the linebacker. If he comes toward the offensive lineman, the offensive lineman blocks with full bench. If he goes over the top, the offensive lineman takes over the down defender.

Coach's Whistle:

- The offensive lineman should not push against his partner. If the defender has attacked the gap and the offensive lineman's partner is steering him up the field, the offensive lineman should give him room and be ready to go to the linebacker.

- If the defender hangs on the offensive lineman's partner, he should be very physical and gore him.

- The offensive lineman shows pass and remains patient letting the defense react.

Bump (Figure 2-27)

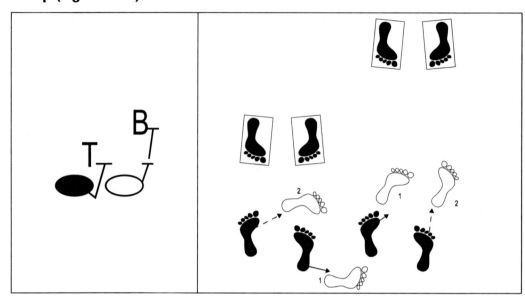

Figure 2-27. Bump: center

Description: This block is used when the center needs help from the guard with a shaded nose.

■ Center

Position: Outside-foot tract

First Step: Pivot with playside foot

Second Step: Crossover with backside foot

Punch: Reach and rip

Mechanics: The center will execute a crossover lunge technique, but he will stay up and run the defender or pin him. The offensive lineman takes pull steps. He uses low pads (shoulder pads as low to the ground as possible) and works through the body of the down defender to rip the playside armpit. The center receives slug help from the frontside guard. If the center reaches the nose, the offensive lineman turns and pins him inside. If the nose runs, the offensive lineman cuts or clips him.

■ Guard

Mechanics: The guard executes a slug block. He must zone step with his inside foot to give the center more room to execute his block. He slugs the shoulder of the down defender to slow him down for the center. The zone step should align the guard on an angle to block the linebacker.

Coach's Whistle:

• The center must stay low on the pull steps. He may have to lose some ground to reach the nose.

- The guard must step with his inside foot to give the center more room to reach the nose. This step must put him on an angle to block the linebacker (visualize/shooting ducks).

Coaching Point

Instruct your players to keep their pads lower than the defender's pads.

Otto Greule/Allsport

The bump block is used when the center needs help from the guard with a shaded nose.

Blunt (Figure 2-28)

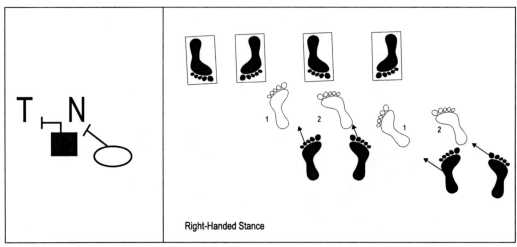

Figure 2-28. Blunt

Description: The center uses blunt to help double-team the nose before blocking back on the down defender over the pulling guard. A coach makes this game plan call for two reasons:

- The nose is a strong player who needs to be double-teamed.
- The down defender is a hat reader and not a penetrator.

■ Center

Position: Inside-foot tract

First Step: Zone with backside foot

Second Step: Zone with playside foot

Landmark: Backside number

Punch: Flipper

Mechanics: The center throws flipper on the second step and swings his body through the nose guard and toward the down defender over the pulling guard. The offensive lineman must not allow penetration in the backside gap.

■ Guard

Mechanics: The guard executes a base block on the nose using a zone step.

Coach's Whistle:

- The center cannot hang onto the nose. He must get back to the down defender on the pulling guard.
- If the down defender aligned on the pulling guard becomes a penetrator, the call becomes "Ollie." The center executes a choke, and the guard base blocks the nose with no help.

Three-Man Combos

When the structure of the defense calls for three-man combination blocks, start with the two two-man combos (slip and scoop) and add a third blocker to form three-man combos: slip becomes skid and scoop becomes slide.

Skid (Figure 2-29)

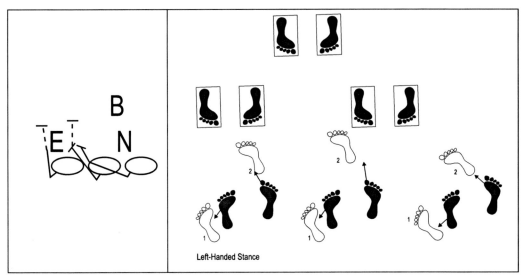

Figure 2-29. Skid

Description: Skid turns a slip block from a two-man combo to a three-man combo. Skid helps pick up a defense that tries to confuse blocking schemes by slanting and pinching.

Mechanics: The two outside blockers will execute a slip block, with a slight alteration: the inside lineman will slug the down defender with his inside hand to help secure the line of scrimmage and to give hand presence to the backside lineman. The backside lineman will execute a two-hand takeover.

Coach's Whistle:

- The lineman must trust his eyes reading the defense on the run.
- The lineman must stay on the duck and trust his partner.

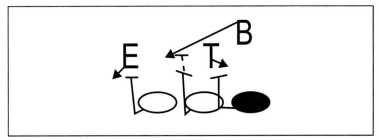

Figure 2-30. Skid—The defensive end takes the Z gap, the linebacker takes the Y gap, and the N takes the X gap. The tackle base blocks because of the defensive end working outside. The guard half-benches the nose and stays on the duck to the linebacker. The center blocks the nose.

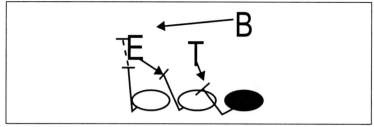

Figure 2-31. Skid—The linebacker takes the Z gap, the defensive end takes the Y gap, and the N takes the X gap. The tackle half benches the defensive end and stays on the duck to the linebacker. The guard base blocks the defensive end. The center blocks the nose.

Slide (Figure 2-32)

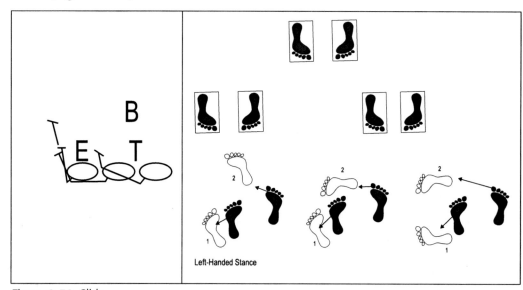

Figure 2-32. Slide

Description: Slide changes scoop from a two-man combo to a three-man combo. Slide can be used to help pick up a defense that tries to confuse blocking schemes by slanting and pinching.

Mechanics: The two outside blockers will execute a scoop block. The backside lineman will execute a crossover lunge or cut. He gets on the correct path and stays on that path. The lineman blocking the linebacker will cut or rip. The tackle's inside foot stays down the midline of the defensive end. Doing so keeps the tackle from stepping around the block.

Coach's Whistle:

- The lineman must stay on the correct path to reach the adjacent down defender.

Coaching Point

The offensive lineman can cut or clip in the line of scrimmage as a change-up to confuse the defense.

Coach's Clipboard

Individual Blocks
- Base
- Base stretch
- Backside cutoff-inside play
- Backside cutoff-outside play
- Cross-over lunge
- Funnel and hinge
- Sift
- Choke
- Reverse hip

Two-Man Combos
- Slip
- Scoop
- Tag
- Tug
- Chip
- Slug
- I'm Gone
- Rub
- Bump
- Blunt

Three-Man Combos
- Skid
- Slide

PASS PROTECTION AND TWIST

Otto Greule Jr./Getty Images

Chapter Three

Pass protection is the make-or-break of the offensive line. In the run game, a coach may "hide" a lesser athlete by putting him in a position where he will have some inside or outside help most of the time. In the pass game, however, linemen are on an "island" (one-on-one with space between them), and must rely on their own skill and talent to be successful. Sometimes double-teams can be created, but if the defense brings the right five rushers, the offensive line has five islands.

A team demonstrates its athleticism in pass protection. The tackles very seldom receive help in pass pro. Tackles must be superior athletes, not only because they are on an island, but because they have the most ground to cover—especially on the open-end side. In professional football, tackles command huge salaries and have become as high as the number-two pick in the draft. Pro teams understand the importance of being able to block the great athletes that play defensive end, and to protect the blind side of the quarterback.

The next most difficult position is center. Snapping the ball leaves the center temporarily one-handed while one hand is between his legs delivering the ball to the quarterback. The center always needs help from the uncovered guard until the blitzer is identified.

Pass protection is easiest for the guards because they have less space to cover; plus, in a four-man rush, one of the guards receives help from the center. The coach may game plan for the center to provide help covering the superior defensive linemen by giving the guard inside help.

This chapter does not cover specific pass protection schemes but it will teach the fundamentals of dropback pass protection. Each lineman must recognize the following four fundamentals:

- The line is responsible for the four down defenders and one linebacker (the ID)
- The defense *always* has one more rusher than the offense can block (the quarterback has never thrown a block in pass protection).
- A lineman must know who the ID is and where he is in the defense.
- A lineman must know if he has help and where it will come from.

By understanding and drilling these aspects, a lineman will be able to use his technique to his advantage, keeping the defenders from having a two-way rush to the quarterback.

Coaching Point

The ID is the linebacker who is assigned to the offensive line
in a specific pass-pro scheme.

The Basics of Pass Protection

It is important for offensive linemen to comprehend the basics of pass protection, which expand upon the four fundamentals.

- The player should know the launch point.

  The offensive lineman always knows where the quarterback is setting up (launch point). This knowledge allows the lineman to position himself properly in relationship to the quarterback and the defender.

- The player should get into the pass set quickly.

  The offensive lineman gets on the bar stool and does not allow the rusher to make contact while he is still in the process of getting into his set. The offensive lineman must remain patient, not committing too soon. He lets the rusher make the first move unless it is an aggressive situation.

- The player should use his hands.

  The offensive lineman must understand the importance of using his hands. The player who establishes inside hand position first almost always wins.

- The player should know his help.

  If the lineman is covered by a down defender, he should always know if he has help, and the direction of the help.

- The player should maintain a relaxed demeanor.

  A relaxed demeanor allows the lineman to keep fundamentally sound and to react to the defender appropriately.

- The player should keep his arches in the ground.

  Any weight shift will make the OL prone to being pulled or bull rushed (pushed back into the quarterback).

- The player should time the punch.

  The lineman's punch should reach its target: the defender. If the lineman punches early, he leaves himself exposed. If he punches too late, he'll lock his hands. Timing the punch provides the power to stop the rusher or to knock him out of his rush lane.

- The player should keep proper position.

  As the punch lands, the head goes back and the butt sinks.

- The player should define the pocket.

  On dropback passes, the center and guards provide the depth of the pocket, and the tackles provide the width of the pocket.

- The player should cover in the direction of the pass.

  After the ball is thrown, the player should cover in the direction of the pass. If the pass is intercepted, "save" the touchdown and give the defense a chance to stop them.

- The player should look for work.

  When not covered by a rusher, the offensive lineman "looks for work." He finds a rusher and gores him.

- The player should inside tract the defender.

  The lineman's shoes stay inside the defender's shoes. The lineman will not see this, but will feel it. His eyes stay up and the lineman maintains an inside presence.

- The player should keep the inside hand strong.

  A strong inside hand prevents a defender from grabbing the outside shoulder.

Basics of a Pass Set

Another important aspect of a successful passing game is getting out of the stance and into a pass set as quickly as possible. The battle is won in the first second of the snap; the winner usually gains foot, body, and hand position.

Key Fundamentals of a Pass Set

- Getting on the barstool

  Head and upper body come up quickly along with the first step (kick or power). These moves all happen as quickly as possible.

- Maintaining correct position

  The butt sinks and the knees remain bent.

- Staying on the arches

  Weight remains over his arches with slightly more weight on his inside foot.

- Maintaining a stagger

  The offensive lineman must be careful not to stagger so much that his weight goes to the heel of his inside foot, creating an unstable base.

- Bringing the hands up

  On the snap, the hands come up. The lineman carries his hands close to his body and keeps his fingertips aligned under his chin. He squeezes his ribs to ensure that his hands do not get too low or too far from his body.

- Relaxing

  The upper body should stay relaxed.

- Maintaining the barstool position

  The lineman's ankle stays outside the knee, and the knee remains outside the hip. If one of these angles is lost, too much weight shifts to that leg.

Basics of Pass Set Steps

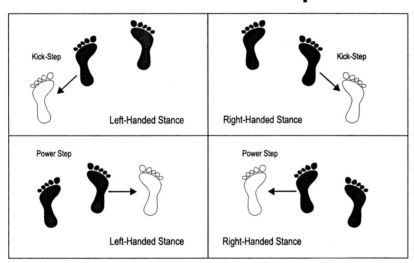

Figure 3-1. Pass-set steps

Pass protection uses only three steps:

- Power

  A power step stops the inside rush. It is a flat, aggressive step with the inside foot. The knee and hip of the inside leg must remain strong and have contact with the down defender.

Coaching Point

The offensive lineman gets into position as if he will trip the down defender with his inside knee. Although he won't actually trip the defender, he puts himself in a position of strength keeping the inside half of his body strong and preventing a "soft shoulder."

- Kick

  A kick step prevents the outside rush. The basic kick step lands at a 45-degree angle. The angle varies with the width of the defender: the wider the defender, the deeper the kick step.

- Slide

  The slide step takes place between a power step or a kick step. It is a short, quick step on the same angle as a power or kick step. In a 1-set the steps are power, slide, power, slide. In a 3-set, the steps are kick, slide, kick, slide.

In pass protection the landmark is the inside number and the body position is inside midline tract, which removes the inside rush lanes (the shortest path to the quarterback). The punch is a perfectly timed short jab using both hands simultaneously. The punch must be timed to keep the weight on the arches and off the toes. The center and the guards are responsible for the depth of the pocket, and maintain this responsibility by keeping their defenders on the line of scrimmage. Tackles are responsible for the width of the pocket by kick stepping and forcing their defenders out of their rush lanes.

The remainder of this chapter demonstrates correct 1-set, 2-set, and 3-set. Ineffective 1- and 3-sets are also covered.

1-Set (Figure 3-2)

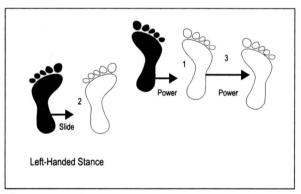

Figure 3-2. 1-Set

Description: The down defender has aligned inside, and the lineman must stop the inside rush.

Position: Inside midline tract

First Step: Power with inside foot

Second Step: Slide with outside foot

Landmark: Inside number

Punch: Two-handed jab

Mechanics: The offensive lineman gets on the bar stool as quickly as possible and power steps to the inside, denying penetration. On the power step, he jams the arch into the ground and slide steps with the outside foot. When done correctly, the lineman feels as if he's tripping the defender with his inside leg and knee. This position of strength will prevent lineman from having a "soft shoulder" (stepping in the bucket opens up the inside lane to the quarterback). The lineman continues to power/slide, flattening the defender down the line of scrimmage toward the boundary and maintaining the integrity of the pocket. Once the defender has committed to the inside rush, the lineman may need to bucket step and run-block the defender out of the cylinder. If the down defender takes an outside rush, the lineman moves from a 1-set to a 3-set. All punches should be timed properly.

Coach's Whistle:

- "Stepping in the bucket" gives the down defender a soft shoulder to rush through, opening up the inside rush lane—the shortest route to the quarterback.

- The offensive lineman should take short steps. If the defender shifts from an inside move to an outside move, the lineman will need to change from a 1-set to a 3-set. Taking big steps makes the conversion impossible. Smaller steps give the lineman the advantage of speed.

- The offensive lineman stays on the bar stool and continues to stick his arches in the ground.

2-Set (Figure 3-3)

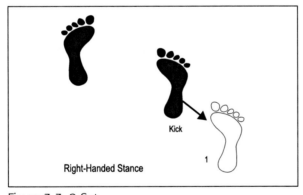

Right-Handed Stance

Kick

1

Figure 3-3. 2-Set

Description: The lineman has perfect inside midline tract position on the down defender. The down defender aligns in an outside-tract position, allowing him to rush either inside or outside.

Position: Inside midline tract

First Step: Kick with outside foot

Second Step: None

Landmark: Inside number

Punch: Two-handed jab

Mechanics: The lineman takes short kick steps with the outside foot and drives the inside knee to the ground (no second step). He is now on the barstool. If the defender rushes inside, the offensive lineman 1-sets; if the defender rushes outside, the offensive lineman 3-sets. Player should time all punches.

Coach's Whistle:

- The lineman must get on the bar stool as quickly as possible, and then react to the rush of the down defender.

3-Set (Figure 3-4)

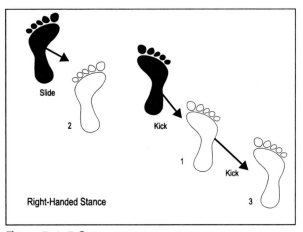

Figure 3-4. 3-Set

Description: The down defender has aligned outside, and the lineman must stop the outside rush.

Position: Inside midline tract

First Step: Kick with outside foot

Second Step: Slide with inside foot

Landmark: Inside number

Punch: Two-handed jab

Mechanics: The kick step must gain width and depth with small steps (player should think 45 degrees and adjust accordingly). The wider the defender, the deeper the kick step, and the more kick/slide steps it will take to establish inside midline-tract position. If the defender goes from an outside rush to an inside rush, adjust from a 3-set to a 1-set. Time all punches.

Coach's Whistle:

- The toes must follow the toes to keep good inside midline tract position.

- Slide steps must be at the same angle. If the slide step is not taken on the same angle as the kick step, the shoulders will turn toward the boundary and create a soft shoulder.

- The offensive lineman must experience a sense of urgency to get on the bar stool, start the kick, and get in position for the block.

Ineffective 1-Set and 3-Set

Offensive linemen must secure the inside rush lane. An inside rush lane that leaves the quarterback open is detrimental to the offense. These common errors should be reviewed with the offensive linemen to prevent this scenario.

A poor power step causes the ineffective 1-set previously mentioned (Figure 3-5). The "step in the bucket" creates a soft shoulder and opens a rush lane to the quarterback.

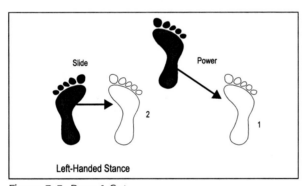

Figure 3-5. Poor 1-Set

A poor slide step creates the ineffective 3-set illustrated in Figure 3-6. The toes must follow the toes. In the diagram, each kick/slide step turns the shoulders more and more, which creates a soft shoulder and opens a rush lane to the quarterback.

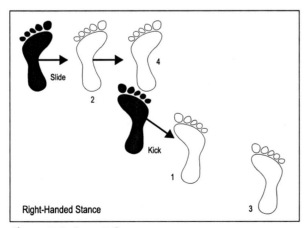

Figure 3-6. Poor 3-Set

Coach's Clipboard

Basics of Pass Pro
- Know the launch point.
- Get into pass set quickly.
- Use the hands.
- Know the help.
- Maintain a relaxed demeanor.
- Keep the arches in the ground.
- Time the punch.
- Keep proper position.
- Define the pocket.
- Cover in the direction of the pass.
- Look for work.
- Inside tract the defender.
- Keep the inside hand strong.

Steps in Pass Pro
- Power
- Kick
- Slide

Fundamentals of a Pass Set
- Get on the barstool.
- Maintain proper position.
- Stay on the arches.
- Maintain a stagger.
- Get hands up.
- Relax.

Pass Sets
- 1-set
- 2-set
- 3-set

1-Set
- Power/slide
- Trip with the inside knee

2-Set
- Get into perfect position.
- Get on the barstool.
- Go to 1-set or 3-set.

3-Set
- Kick/slide
- Toes follow toes

Ineffective 1-Set
- Stepping in the bucket

Ineffective 3-Set
- Slide step doesn't follow kick step

BLOCKING TWIST

Grant Halverson/Getty Images

Chapter Four

The offensive line must know how to block a twist. Coaches should teach the basics of a twist—including its components and how to identify it. This chapter covers those basics and includes:

- Twist pick-up center and guard combinations
- Twist pick-up guard and tackle combinations
- Tackle-nose and nose-tackle twist with frontside linebacker identification
- Tackle-nose and nose-tackle twist with backside linebacker identification
- Tackle-tackle twist with middle linebacker identification
- End-tackle and tackle-end twist

Twist Identification and Characteristics

As a general rule, the offensive line stops a twist by zone blocking. Man blocking of a twist occurs under two conditions:

- By assignment

  Lineman are assigned a specific man

- Different levels

  Linemen are zone blocking but get on different levels and cannot switch off to a different rusher.

Coaches can use the tendencies of the defense to assist with twist blocking. Game plan, down-and-distance, and pre-snap looks can help determine twist possibilities. For example:

- Game plan

  Some defenses may twist by down-and-distance, formations, or against a two-minute offense.

- Down-and-distance

  Some defenses twist only on third down, others on any down when the distance to go is seven yards or more.

- Pre-snap looks

  When the defensive tackle and end have lined up closer together, they are likely to twist. A defensive tackle that aligns tight on the guard and a loose defensive end are less likely to twist because of the distance between them.

  Linemen can identify twist by two components: the penetrator and the looper. To help identify each twist in the diagrams, the first letter represents the penetrator and the second letter indicates the looper in each twist. For example, in the diagram of the end-tackle twist, the end is the penetrator and the tackle is the looper.

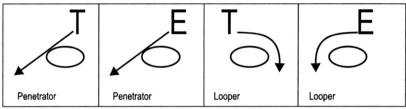

Figure 4-1. Penetrator and looper examples

Characteristics of a Penetrator

- The penetrator tries to grab the lineman more than he tries to rush the quarterback.
- The penetrator moves first toward the blocker, who has the looper, and then toward the quarterback.
- The penetrator's first job is to free the looper.

Characteristics of a Looper

- The looper shows his hands and numbers by standing taller.
- His first steps are usually more deliberate and under control, rather than full speed.
- He looks in the direction of the penetrator to know when to start his loop.

Offensive players must learn the variations of twist based on alignment of the defense. The following twist section will help teach the twist variations by identifying the initial sets and the reaction to the twist.

Twist Pick-Up Center and Guards

Tackle-Nose Twists Versus Frontside Linebacker Identification (Figure 4-2)

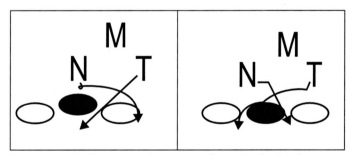

Figure 4-2. Tackle-nose twists versus frontside linebacker identification

The center is helping the guard. The right guard knows he has inside help from the center because of the alignment of the linebacker.

Initial Sets:

- Right guard: 3-sets with inside help from the center.

- Center: Center 3-sets to linebacker, and punches the nose guard with his near hand as he sets. (This approach is called" dragging off the nose.")
- Left guard: Left guard 1-sets with no help from the center. The guard must protect the center because his 3-set turns him away from the nose.

If the defense runs a tackle-nose twist, the offensive line reacts as follows:

- Right guard: As the tackle penetrates, he hands the defender to the center with his inside hand, looks inside for the looper and the linebacker, and blocks the looper.
- Center: Blocks the tackle.
- Left guard: As the nose starts to loop, he sinks (gets depth) and looks in the direction of the looper for the linebacker or looper. If the linebacker blitzes toward the left guard, the guard blocks him. If no blitzer, the left guard looks for work.

If the defense runs a nose-tackle twist, the offensive line reacts as follows:

- Right guard: As the tackle starts to loop, the right guard sinks and looks for the linebacker. If the linebacker blitzes, the right guard blocks him. If the linebacker drops, the guard looks for work.
- Center: Sets and spots the looper. He attacks the gap in the direction of the looper, and he blocks the nose.
- Left guard: As the nose penetrates, the left guard flattens him, preventing him from reaching the center's inside shoulder. The guard blocks him and hands him off to the center. He looks for the looper and blocks the looper.

Tackle-Nose Twists Versus Back Side Linebacker Identification (Figure 4-3)

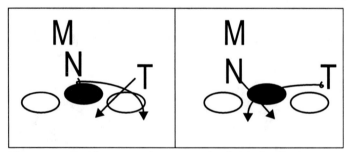

Figure 4-3. Tackle-nose twists versus backside linebacker identification

Initial Sets:

- Right guard: 2-sets to the tackle with no help from the center
- Center: 2-sets to the nose and puts eyes on the linebacker.
- Left guard: 1-sets to the nose with his eyes on the linebacker, knowing he has help from the center.

If the defense runs a tackle-nose twist, the offensive line reacts as follows:

- Right guard: Moves from a 2-set to a 1-set and hands the tackle off to the center, sinks and looks for the looper.

- Center: As the nose starts his loop, the center gets eyes in the direction of the looper and blocks the tackle. The center can block the penetrator in two ways:

   ✓ 1-set and bump the right guard off.

   ✓ Bucket step and attack the penetrator.

- Left guard: As the nose starts to loop, he puts his eyes on the linebacker. If the linebacker blitzes, the left guard blocks him. If the linebacker starts his pass drop, the left guard sinks and looks for work.

If the defense runs a nose-tackle twist, the offensive line reacts as follows:

- Right guard: As the tackle starts to loop, the right guard puts his eyes on the linebacker. If the linebacker blitzes, the guard blocks him. If the linebacker starts his pass drop, the guard sinks and looks for work.

- Center: As the nose penetrates toward the center, the center blocks him.

- Left guard: As the nose penetrates, the left guard punches him with his inside hand and hands him off to the center, keeping his eyes on the linebacker. If the linebacker blitzes, the left guard blocks him. If the linebacker starts his pass drop, the left guard sinks and helps the center.

Tackle-Tackle Twists Versus Middle Linebacker Identification (Figure 4-4)

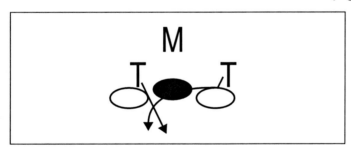

Figure 4-4. Tackle twist versus middle linebacker identification

Initial Sets:

- Right guard: Sets according to the alignment of the defensive tackle (for example, 3-sets against a loose tackle, and 1-sets against a tight tackle).

- Center: Sets to the depth of the two guards, in the middle of the two defensive tackles with his eyes on the linebacker. For example, if a loose technique tackle is on the rightside and a tight technique tackle on the leftside, the center sets slightly to the right.

- Left guard: Sets according to the alignment of the defensive tackle (for example, 3-sets against a loose tackle, and 1-sets against a tight tackle).

If the defense runs a tackle-tackle twist, the offensive line reacts as follows:

- Right guard: As the tackle starts his loop, the guard looks in the direction of the looper for the linebacker. If the linebacker blitzes, the guard blocks him. If the linebacker starts his pass drop, the guard sinks and looks for work.

- Center: Sets for depth, which keeps him from getting "picked" by a penetrating tackle. He keeps his eyes on the linebacker. If the linebacker blitzes to the center, the center blocks him. If the linebacker blitzes around one of the guards, the center knocks the guard off and blocks the tackle.

- Left guard: As the tackle starts to penetrate, the left guard moves to a 1-set and flattens the tackle, and the center knocks the guard off the block and takes over the tackle. The left guard must keep his eyes on the linebacker. If the linebacker blitzes, the left guard blocks him. If the linebacker starts his pass drop, the left guard looks for work.

Twist Pick-Up: Guard and Tackle

End-Tackle Twist (Figure 4-5)

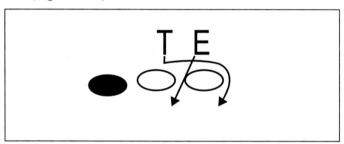

Figure 4-5. End-tackle twist

Initial Sets:

- Guard: Sets according to the technique of the defensive tackle (for example, if facing a loose technique tackle, 3-sets, if facing a normal technique, 2-sets, or if facing a tight technique, 1-sets).

- Tackle: If the defensive end is in a normal alignment, 3-sets. If the end is tighter than normal, he 2-sets him and looks for the twist.

If the defense runs an end-tackle twist:

- Guard: As the defensive tackle starts his loop, the guard always looks in the direction of the looper and attacks the penetrator. The offensive tackle will not recognize the twist until the guard makes contact and knocks him onto the looper. On contact, the guard run blocks the penetrator and tries to create a pile in case the tackle is grabbed.

- Tackle: As the end starts to penetrate, the tackle moves to a 1-set and flattens him into the guard. The tackle should anticipate being knocked onto the looper. As the tackle comes off the penetrator, he sets for a little depth and blocks the looper.

Tackle-End Twist (Figure 4-6)

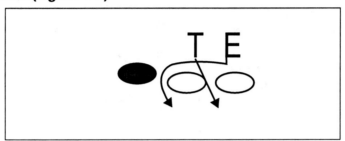

Figure 4-6. Tackle-end twist

Initial Sets:

- Guard: Sets according to the technique of the defensive tackle (for example if it is a loose-technique tackle, 3-sets, if a normal technique, 2-sets, and if tight technique, 1-sets).

- Tackle: If the defensive end is in a normal alignment, 3-set. If the end is tighter than normal, 2-sets, and looks for the twist.

If the defense runs a tackle-end twist:

- Guard: As the penetrator works up the field, the guard times his punch and flattens the penetrator. The guard feels the rush angle of the penetrator and notes if he is working his rush lane, or if he is trying to pick the tackle. The guard flattens the penetrator across the face of his tackle. The guard stays on the penetrator until he feels the tackle and then blocks the looper.

- Tackle: As the defensive end starts to loop, the tackle bucket steps and attacks in the direction of the looper, knocking his guard off the penetrator onto the looper. On contact with the defender, he run blocks the penetrator and tries to create a pile in case the guard has been grabbed.

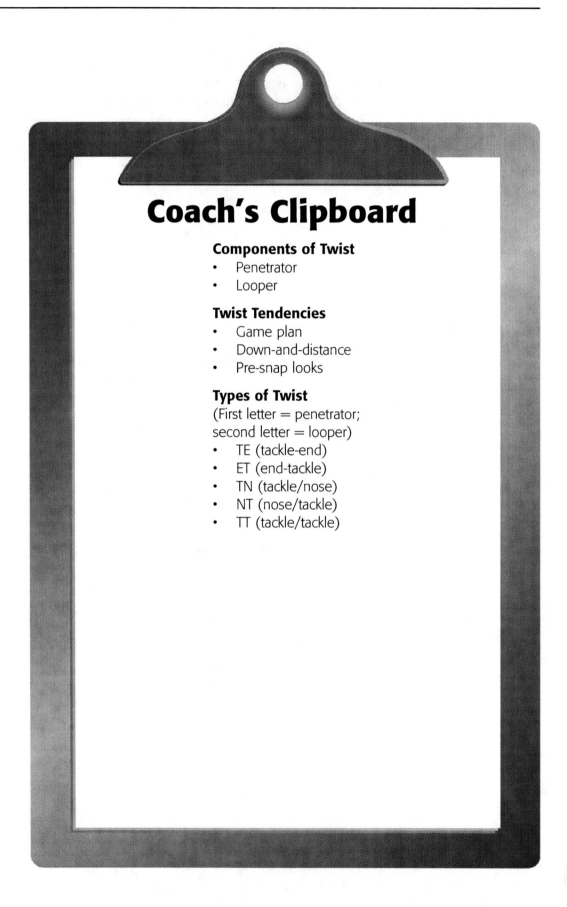

Coach's Clipboard

Components of Twist
- Penetrator
- Looper

Twist Tendencies
- Game plan
- Down-and-distance
- Pre-snap looks

Types of Twist
(First letter = penetrator;
second letter = looper)
- TE (tackle-end)
- ET (end-tackle)
- TN (tackle/nose)
- NT (nose/tackle)
- TT (tackle/tackle)

PASS COMBOS

Stephen Dunn/Getty Images

Chapter Five

The first question a lineman must ask himself in pass protection is, "Do I have any help?" The answer to this question determines how the lineman reacts when he has either inside or outside help against a range of defensive looks. These pass combinations involve two or three offensive linemen who are responsible for the same number of defenders in a specific defensive look. Pass combos are based on the fundamentals of pass protection: 1-, 2-, and 3-set.

Coaches can expand the lineman's repertoire with the introduction of jump sets covered in this chapter. In a jump set, the lineman changes his "sitting on the barstool" set to an aggressive set that catches the defender off guard. A jump set forces the defender to counter a completely different pass set. The change requires the defender to think (instead of reacting immediately), slowing his pass rush, and giving an advantage to the offensive line.

Center and Guards Versus Even Defense (Figure 5-1)

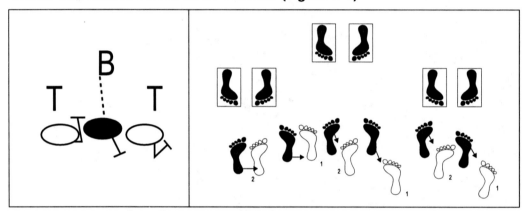

Figure 5-1. Center and guards versus even defense

In this pass combination, the guards must know if the center is setting in the middle of the guards, or to one side or the other. The center covers the inside gap (or gaps) and the linebacker.

If the linebacker blitzes, the center must block the linebacker, or switch with the guard to cover the side of the blitz. If a guard knows that he has inside help from the center, he can overset the defender to take away the outside rush, making the defender think he has a free inside rush. The center sits inside, waiting on the defender's move, and the guard restricts the center's assigned space, creating an easy pick-up for the center.

The guard that has no help from the center must 1-set (set to take away the inside move), forcing the defender to make an outside rush to the quarterback.

If the center sets in the middle of the two guards, he offers help to both of them. The guards can overset to the outside, forcing the defender to take the inside rush. If this happens, the guards must 1-set inside until they feel the center's help. By knowing where the center's help comes from, the guards can dictate the rush of the defenders.

Guards

3-set to the outside number of the tackle (because of help from the center).

- If the tackle works outside, guards block tackle one-on-one and think, "No help from the center."
- If the tackle works inside, guards start to 1-set and stay on the tackle unless the center bumps the guard off. If the center bumps the guard off, the guard looks for the blitzing linebacker.
- If the tackle becomes the looper, guards look for the blitzing linebacker. If no blitz, sink for depth and help on the twist.

Center

3-sets for depth and equal distance between the two defensive tackles. Keeps his eyes on the linebacker.

- If the linebacker stays, the center looks for work and gores someone.
- If the linebacker blitzes toward the center, the center takes the linebacker.
- If the linebacker blitzes toward the guard, the center bumps him off and blocks the tackle.

On a tackle-tackle twist, the center attacks in the direction of the looper. Doing so puts the center on the penetrator and frees his guard to block the looper.

Center and Guards Versus Guard Stack (Figure 5-2)

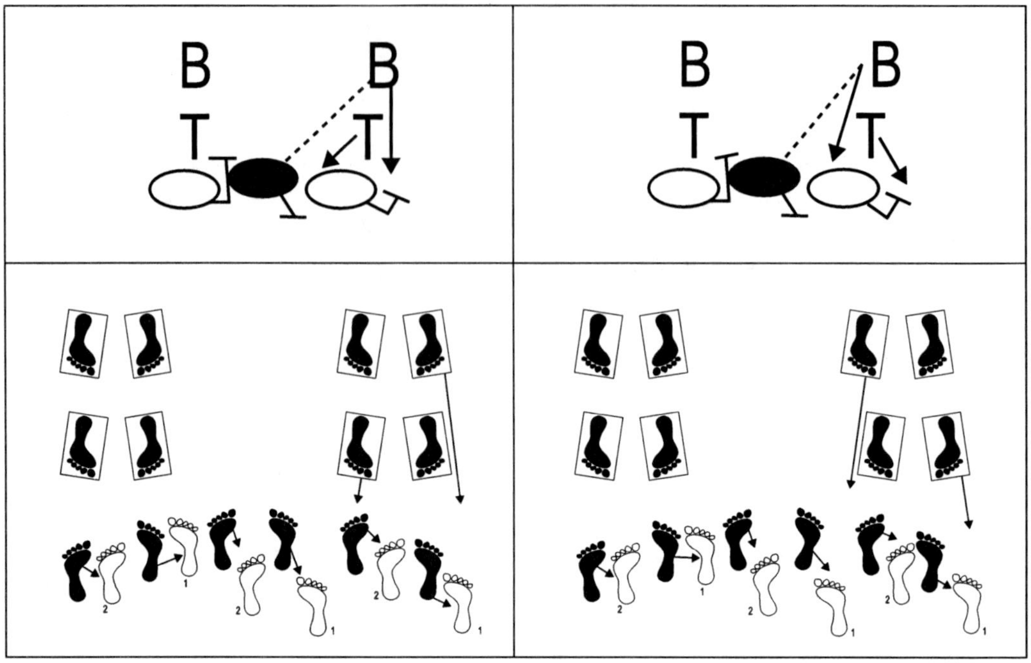

Figure 5-2. Center and guards versus guard stack

In this look, the center definitely works to one side or the other. The guard with help can overset, but he must be ready to switch with the center in case the linebacker blitzes. The guard away from the help must 1-set to protect the inside rush. If the linebacker to the side away from the center's help threatens the A gap, the guard should "down" the gap and block the linebacker, letting the back block the down defender.

Coaching Point

Down is not a line call, but a reaction by the guard at the line of scrimmage on the snap of the ball. The "down" protects the A gap or the X gap. The guard should decide whether the linebacker poses a threat in the gap based on his ability to run through and sack the quarterback. The back in pass protection should see his linebacker as a threat in the gap and watch the guard, blocking the man the guard releases.

Frontside Guard

3-sets to the outside number of the tackle (because of help from the center).

- If the tackle works outside, the frontside guard takes the tackle one-on-one and thinks, "No help from the center."

- If the tackle works inside, he keeps outside leverage on the tackle (the center will block the tackle), and looks for the blitzing linebacker.

- If the tackle becomes the looper, he looks for the blitzing linebacker. If no blitz, sinks for depth and help on the twist.

Backside Guard

1-sets the tackle (because of no help from the center).

- If the center bumps him off, backside guard thinks twist and looks for the looper.
- If the tackle becomes the looper, he looks for the blitzing linebacker.
- If no blitz, he sinks for depth and helps on the twist.

Center

3-sets with width and depth to his frontside guard keeping his eyes on the linebacker.

- If the linebacker stays, the center looks for work and gores someone.
- If the linebacker blitzes toward the center, the center blocks him.
- If the linebacker blitzes toward the guard, the center bumps him off and blocks the tackle.

On a tackle-tackle twist, the center attacks in the direction of the looper. Doing so puts him on the penetrator, and frees the guard to block the looper.

Center and Guard Versus Noseguard and Onside Linebacker and Covered Guard (Figure 5-3)

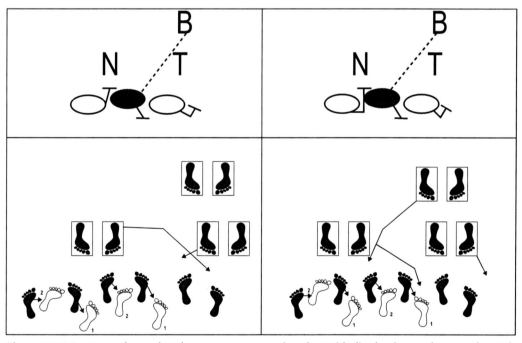

Figure 5-3. Center and guard tech versus noseguard and outside linebacker and covered guard

In this look (and the two variations that follow), the center's job is a difficult one: if the nose works away from his help and the linebacker blitzes, the center must take over the nose without help. The center should slightly overset the nose to try to force him into the inside rush to the guard who is helping. Oversetting puts the center in great blocking position in case the nose rushes away from the guard. The uncovered guard who is responsible for the linebacker should always set to the nose, protecting the center while keeping his eye on the linebacker.

Coaching Point

In pass protection, if a lineman sets to a down defender and the down defender disappears, the lineman should get depth (sink). For example, if a guard sets to the nose (1-set) and the nose disappears, the guard stops the 1-set and starts getting depth off the line of scrimmage. Sinking protects the guard from getting picked by a looper and keeps him on the same level as the other linemen. Remember: if a defender disappears, someone is coming back to take his place.

Frontside Guard

3-set to the outside number of the tackle (because of help from the center).

- If the tackle works outside, the frontside guard takes the tackle one-on-one and thinks, "No help from the center."
- If the tackle works inside, the guard keeps outside leverage on the tackle (the center will block the tackle), and looks for the blitzing linebacker.
- If the tackle becomes the looper, the guard looks for the blitzing linebacker.
- If no blitz, the guard sinks for depth and helps on the twist.

Backside Guard

Bucket steps and sets aggressively to the nose with a slight turn of hips and shoulders (pees on his foot), and aggressively punches the nose (gores him) if the defender hangs on the center.

- If the linebacker stays, the center will stay and help. He should think, "No help."
- If the nose works away, the guard sinks for depth and anticipates the linebacker or a twist.

Center

3-sets with width and depth to his frontside guard. Center punches the nose with his backside hand as he sets. He keeps his eyes on the linebacker. The center should think, "Twist," and avoid getting picked.

- If the nose works away, the center anticipates a linebacker blitz. If he comes, the center stones him.
- If the nose works toward the center and the linebacker blitzes the backside, the center takes over the nose and bumps the guard off to block the linebacker.
- If no blitz, the center looks for work and gores someone.

Center and Guard Versus Noseguard and Onside Linebacker (Figure 5-4)

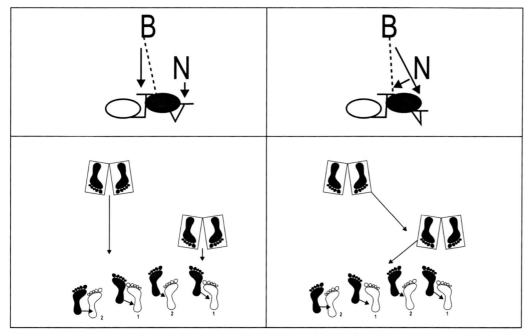

Figure 5-4. Center and guard versus noseguard and onside linebacker

Guard

1-sets to a position next to the center, keeping his shoulders square.

- If the linebacker stays and the nose comes toward the guard, he takes half and maintains his stagger.
- If the linebacker stays and the nose works away, the guard gets depth and thinks, "Twist." If no twist, he gores someone.
- If the linebacker blitzes to the guard, the guard blocks him.
- If the linebacker blitzes away, the guard bumps the center off and takes over the nose.

Center

3-sets to the outside number of the nose. Doing so takes the rush lane away from the center's help. The center jams the nose.

- If the nose works toward the center, the center stays on him and flattens him, thinking, "No help."
- If the nose works away, the center looks for the linebacker.
- If the linebacker stays, the center squeezes his half of the nose.
- If the linebacker blitzes, the center blocks him.

Fan (Figure 5-5)

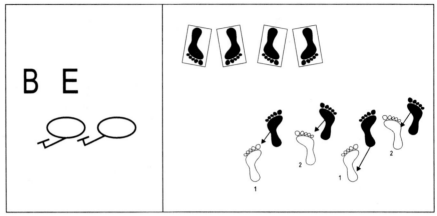

Figure 5-5. Fan

In this guard/tackle combo, one defender lines up head-up and another defender lines up outside the tackle. The tackle makes this call on the line of scrimmage upon recognition of the defense. In this look, the tackle must change up his set to protect against any crossing stunts by the defense. This look is a very popular look for defenses, therefore time is very well spent in practice picking up the various looks and blitzes the defense can execute out of this look.

Guard

3-sets for width, anticipating the defensive tackle pinching down inside. Too much depth will allow the defensive tackle to have an outside shoulder edge to the quarterback, destroying the depth of the pocket. If the defensive tackle takes an outside rush to the tackle, the guard looks for twist. If no twist, he works inside and helps the center.

Tackle

3-sets for depth. He puts his eyes on the defensive end, and feels the rush of the defensive tackle. If the tackle gets a tackle-end twist, he must be in position to block the defensive tackle.

Coach's Whistle:

- If the tackle sets for too much width and a tackle-end twist occurs, the defensive tackle will be on the tackle's inside shoulder and will have an inside rush to the quarterback.

Gate (Figure 5-6)

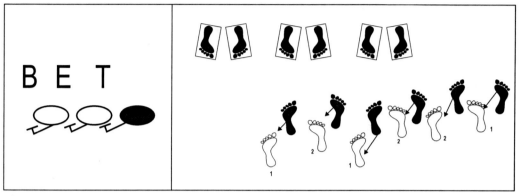

Figure 5-6. Gate

Gate is a center, guard, and tackle pick-up versus another very popular defensive look. It is basically the same as the fan look, except the guard is covered. This look includes two defensive linemen and a linebacker. The linemen call the gate on the line of scrimmage upon recognition of the defense. The call turns the protection pick-up from a man scheme to a zone scheme, where the center covers the X gap, the guard covers the Y gap, and the tackle covers the Z gap. If a lineman's gap remains open, the free lineman should help his partners by finding someone to gore.

Center

3-sets to the inside half of the defensive tackle, anticipating a pinch by the defensive tackle. If the defensive tackle disappears, the center stops his set and looks for a looper coming toward him.

Guard

3-sets for width, anticipating that the defensive end will pinch down inside. Too much depth will allow the defensive end to have an outside shoulder edge to the quarterback and destroy the depth of the pocket. If the defensive end takes an outside rush to the tackle, guard should look for twist. If no twist, he should work back inside and help the center.

Tackle

3-sets for depth, putting his eyes on the linebacker, and feeling the rush of the defensive end. In case of an end-backer twist, the tackle must be in position to block the defensive end.

Coach's Whistle:

- This scheme is a gap pick-up scheme, therefore the set to the gap is of utmost importance. Any over set will widen the gap and make it harder to pick up a twist.

Sort (Figure 5-7)

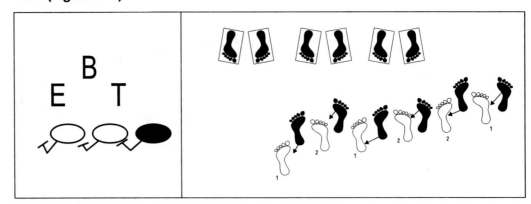

Figure 5-7. Sort

This front is another center, guard and tackle pick-up versus a common defensive front. In sort (which is similar to gate), the linebacker starts in a stack position behind the down defenders. The linemen call sort on the line of scrimmage upon recognition of the defense. With a gate call, sort turns the protection pick-up from a man scheme to a zone scheme, where the center covers the X gap, the guard covers the Y gap, and the tackle covers the Z gap. If a lineman's gap remains open, the free lineman should help his partners by finding someone to gore.

Center

3-sets to the playside gap and scans from the triangle (defensive tackle, defensive end, and linebacker). The center blocks the blitzer that shows in the gap. If no blitzer, the center looks for work.

Guard

2-sets to the playside gap and scans the triangle. The guard blocks the blitzer that shows in the gap. The center will take anyone to the inside gap.

Tackle

3-sets for depth. He puts his eyes on the defensive end and feels the rush of the defensive tackle. In the event of a tackle-end twist, the tackle must be in position to block the defensive tackle. The guard will take anyone to the inside gap.

Coach's Whistle:

- This scheme is a gap-protection scheme. The guard and tackle have inside help; they cannot chase a defender that crosses their face.

Coach's Clipboard

Guard and Tackle Pick-Up
- Fan

Center, Guard, and Tackle Pick-Up
- Gate
- Sort

Center and Guard Combos
- Versus even defense
- Versus guard stack
- Versus nose and inside linebacker
- Versus slide defense

BLOCKING SCHEMES

Chapter Six

Once players master the fundamentals of the offensive line and successfully execute the blocks covered in this manual, coaches and players may hesitate to transfer this information and skills to the various looks they will encounter against defenses. This chapter matches the blocks with runs in certain defensive looks to show where the individual and combination blocks fit in these schemes. The chapter includes the most popular running game plays from a variety of offenses. The blocking schemes demonstrate one suggested manner for blocking the various defensive looks. These plays should be considered as starting points that coaches adjust to match their personnel and beliefs. The blocking schemes highlight six of the most popular defensive fronts. All other fronts are variations of these six.

David Maxwell/Getty Images

A blocking scheme involves a coach's effort to match his personnel and beliefs to block a specific defensive look on a particular play.

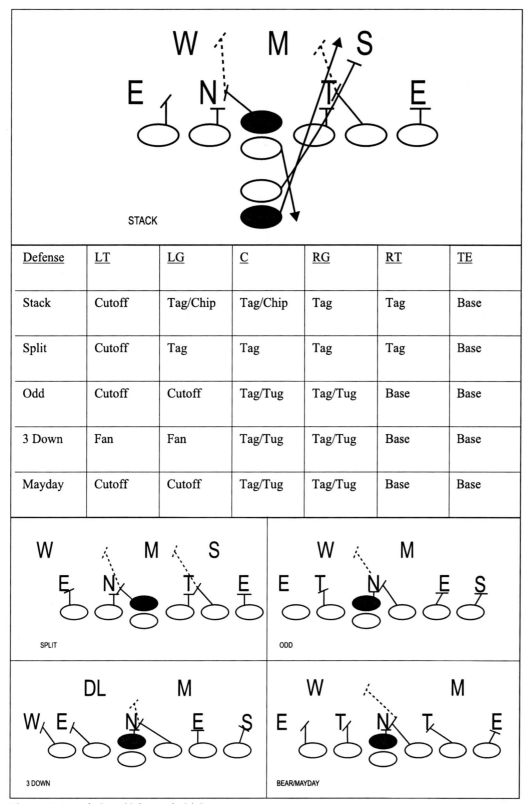

Defense	LT	LG	C	RG	RT	TE
Stack	Cutoff	Tag/Chip	Tag/Chip	Tag	Tag	Base
Split	Cutoff	Tag	Tag	Tag	Tag	Base
Odd	Cutoff	Cutoff	Tag/Tug	Tag/Tug	Base	Base
3 Down	Fan	Fan	Tag/Tug	Tag/Tug	Base	Base
Mayday	Cutoff	Cutoff	Tag/Tug	Tag/Tug	Base	Base

Figure 6-1. Isolation (tight end side)

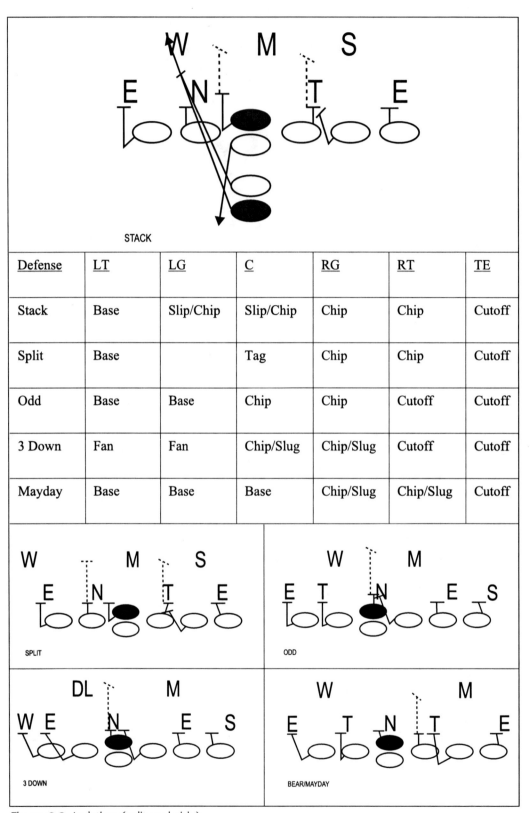

Defense	LT	LG	C	RG	RT	TE
Stack	Base	Slip/Chip	Slip/Chip	Chip	Chip	Cutoff
Split	Base		Tag	Chip	Chip	Cutoff
Odd	Base	Base	Chip	Chip	Cutoff	Cutoff
3 Down	Fan	Fan	Chip/Slug	Chip/Slug	Cutoff	Cutoff
Mayday	Base	Base	Base	Chip/Slug	Chip/Slug	Cutoff

Figure 6-2. Isolation (split end side)

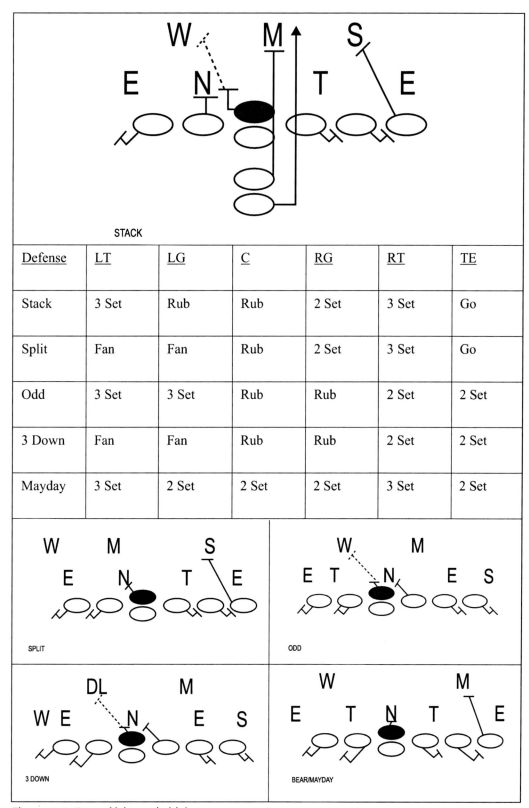

STACK

Defense	LT	LG	C	RG	RT	TE
Stack	3 Set	Rub	Rub	2 Set	3 Set	Go
Split	Fan	Fan	Rub	2 Set	3 Set	Go
Odd	3 Set	3 Set	Rub	Rub	2 Set	2 Set
3 Down	Fan	Fan	Rub	Rub	2 Set	2 Set
Mayday	3 Set	2 Set	2 Set	2 Set	3 Set	2 Set

SPLIT

ODD

3 DOWN

BEAR/MAYDAY

Figure 6-3. Draw (tight end side)

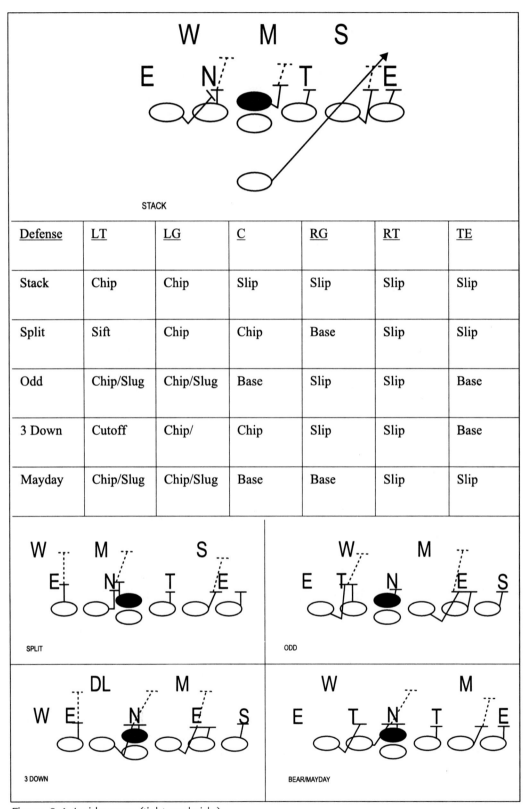

Defense	LT	LG	C	RG	RT	TE
Stack	Chip	Chip	Slip	Slip	Slip	Slip
Split	Sift	Chip	Chip	Base	Slip	Slip
Odd	Chip/Slug	Chip/Slug	Base	Slip	Slip	Base
3 Down	Cutoff	Chip/	Chip	Slip	Slip	Base
Mayday	Chip/Slug	Chip/Slug	Base	Base	Slip	Slip

Figure 6-4. Inside zone (tight end side)

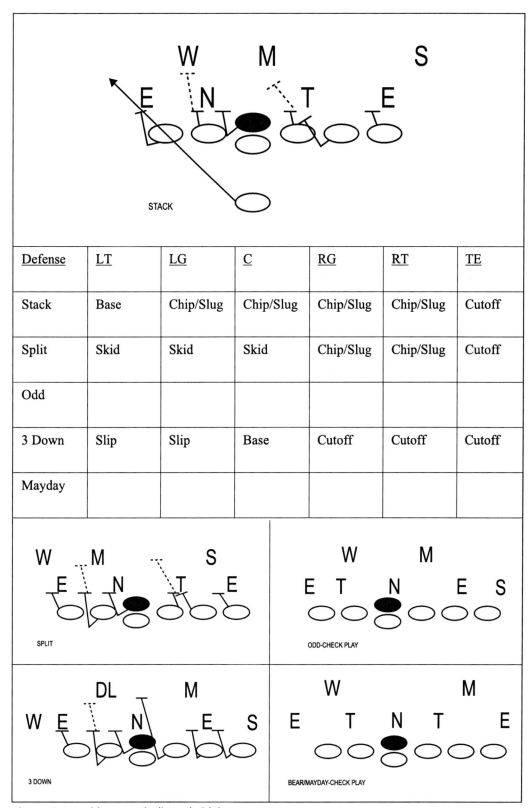

Defense	LT	LG	C	RG	RT	TE
Stack	Base	Chip/Slug	Chip/Slug	Chip/Slug	Chip/Slug	Cutoff
Split	Skid	Skid	Skid	Chip/Slug	Chip/Slug	Cutoff
Odd						
3 Down	Slip	Slip	Base	Cutoff	Cutoff	Cutoff
Mayday						

Figure 6-5. Inside zone (split end side).

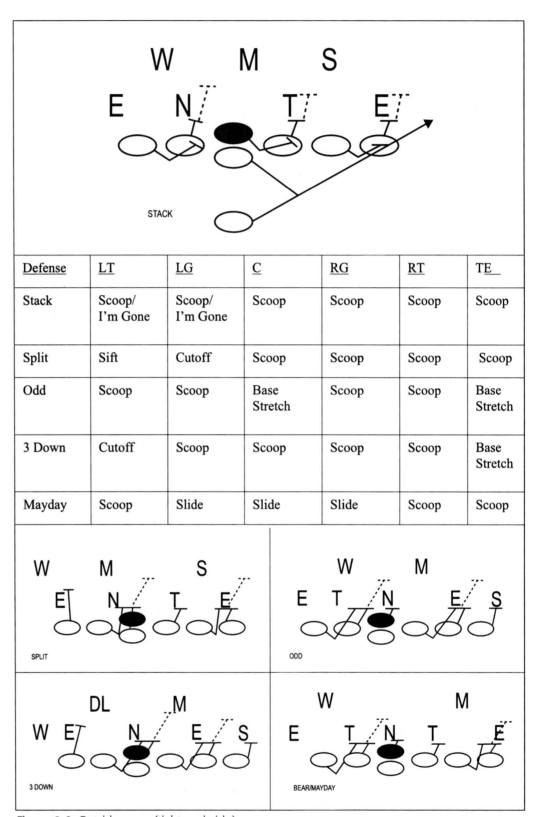

Defense	LT	LG	C	RG	RT	TE
Stack	Scoop/ I'm Gone	Scoop/ I'm Gone	Scoop	Scoop	Scoop	Scoop
Split	Sift	Cutoff	Scoop	Scoop	Scoop	Scoop
Odd	Scoop	Scoop	Base Stretch	Scoop	Scoop	Base Stretch
3 Down	Cutoff	Scoop	Scoop	Scoop	Scoop	Base Stretch
Mayday	Scoop	Slide	Slide	Slide	Scoop	Scoop

Figure 6-6. Outside zone (tight end side)

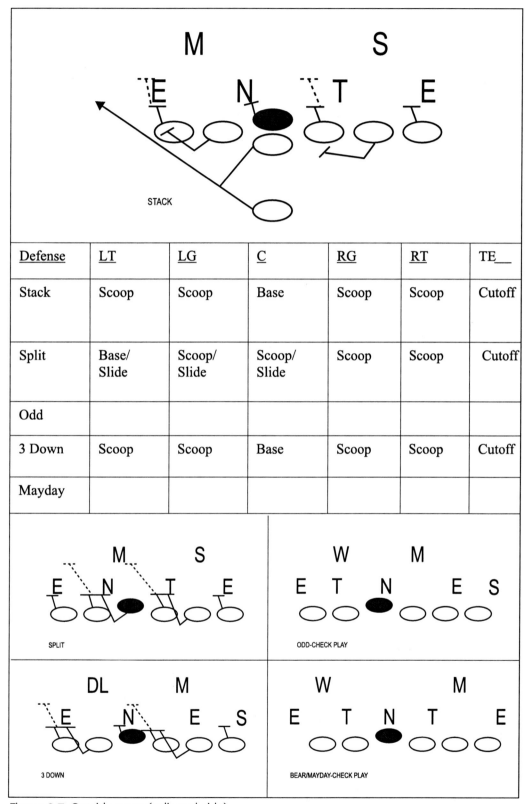

Defense	LT	LG	C	RG	RT	TE__
Stack	Scoop	Scoop	Base	Scoop	Scoop	Cutoff
Split	Base/Slide	Scoop/Slide	Scoop/Slide	Scoop	Scoop	Cutoff
Odd						
3 Down	Scoop	Scoop	Base	Scoop	Scoop	Cutoff
Mayday						

Figure 6-7. Outside zone (split end side)

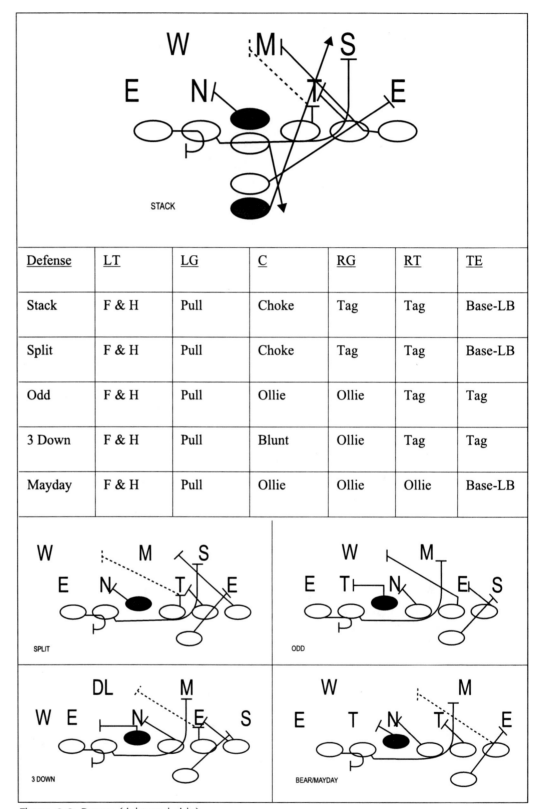

Defense	LT	LG	C	RG	RT	TE
Stack	F & H	Pull	Choke	Tag	Tag	Base-LB
Split	F & H	Pull	Choke	Tag	Tag	Base-LB
Odd	F & H	Pull	Ollie	Ollie	Tag	Tag
3 Down	F & H	Pull	Blunt	Ollie	Tag	Tag
Mayday	F & H	Pull	Ollie	Ollie	Ollie	Base-LB

Figure 6-8. Power (tight end side)

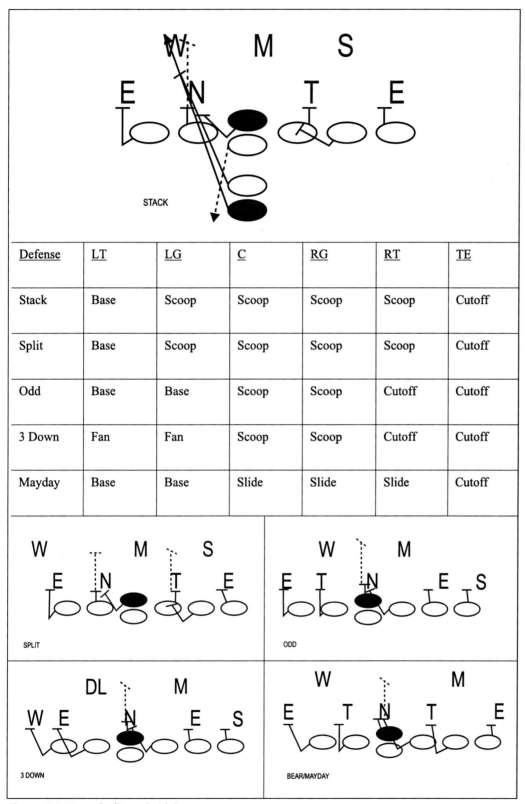

Defense	LT	LG	C	RG	RT	TE
Stack	Base	Scoop	Scoop	Scoop	Scoop	Cutoff
Split	Base	Scoop	Scoop	Scoop	Scoop	Cutoff
Odd	Base	Base	Scoop	Scoop	Cutoff	Cutoff
3 Down	Fan	Fan	Scoop	Scoop	Cutoff	Cutoff
Mayday	Base	Base	Slide	Slide	Slide	Cutoff

Figure 6-9. Toss (split end side)

About the Author

Tim Nunez is a 32-year veteran of collegiate coaching. Over his career, Nunez has coached at the University of Texas, Marshall University, Southwest Texas Sate, Tulane University, and Texas A&M.

Coach Nunez's career highlights include a five-year stint as offensive line coach at the University of Texas, where he directed an offensive line that featured an outland trophy finalist, seven All-Americans, and six first-team All-Big 12 performers. Nunez's line helped the Longhorns offense become only the second offense in NCAA history to feature a 2,000-yard passer and rusher to go along with a 1,000-yard receiver in 1998. The University of Texas offense was one of only four units nationally (first in school history) to feature a 3,000-yard passer, a 1,000-yard receiver, and a 1,000-yard rusher in 1999. Nunez's unit also has cleared room for 16 200-yard rushing games, including a 434-yard rushing effort against Rice in 1998 and a 396-yard ground game at Kansas in 2000.

In 1998, Nunez directed a group of seniors to one of the most productive seasons on record at the University of Texas. He followed that up in 1999 by grooming a Longhorns line that featured four new starters—all underclassmen—who paved the way for another highly productive offense.

In 2000, the University of Texas's offensive line cleared the way for a third consecutive 1,000-yard rusher, and helped the Longhorns gel into a group that ran for 201 yards per game over their final six games of the regular season. Nunez trained a line that was led by Leonard Davis, an outland trophy finalist and a consensus first-team All-American.

Tackle Mike Williams earned first-team All-American and All-Big 12 honors in leading a line that set the stage for Cedric Benson to set a freshman record with 1,053 rushing yards and 12 touchdowns in 2001. In 2002, guard Derrick Dockery earned first-team All-American honors and was an outland trophy semifinalist as he helped pave the way for Benson to rush for 1,247 yards.

Prior to Texas, Nunez coordinated an explosive offense at Marshall during the 1997 season. Under his guidance, Marshall's offense ranked fifth nationally in scoring (37.8 points per game), seventh in passing (307.3 yard per game), and tenth in total offense (444.9 yards per game) as the Thundering Herd won the Mid-American Conference championship.

Marshall wide receiver Randy Moss and quarterback Chad Pennington flourished in Nunez's system in 1997. Moss set an NCAA record for touchdown catches in a season (25) and went on to earn first-team All-American honors. He also finished fourth in the Heisman Trophy balloting. Meanwhile, Pennington led the nation and set the NCAA sophomore record for touchdown passes (39) that season.

A 32-year coaching veteran, Nunez tutored an offensive line that had all of its starters named to the All-Southern Conference team, and helped Marshall claim the Division I-AA national championship in 1996.

Before Marshall, Nunez had coaching stints at Southwest Texas State and Tulane. He served as the Bobcats' assistant head coach/offensive coordinator from 1992–95 and helped SWT lead the Southland Conference in rushing offense in 1992.

At Tulane, Nunez guided the Green Wave's wide receivers from 1988–91 and the secondary/defensive ends from 1984–86.

Nunez attended Louisiana Tech from 1967–68 before going on to earn a degree in health and physical education from Lamar University in 1970. He then earned his Master's in education from Lamar University in 1974.

Tim and Ellen Nunez have five children: Dwayne, Jake, Jame, Mark, and Lori.

For more tips on offensive line techniques and fundamentals from Coach Nunez, visit www.o-lineiscool.com.